Rose Marie

ANTIQUES
OF SPORT

Also by Jerry E. Patterson

Autographs: A Collector's Guide
A Collector's Guide to Relics & Memorabilia

By JERRY E. PATTERSON

ANTIQUES OF SPORT

Crown Publishers, Inc.   New York

Inquiries should be addressed to Crown Publishers, Inc.,
419 Park Avenue South, New York, N.Y. 10016

Printed in the United States of America.

Published simultaneously in Canada by General Publishing Company
Limited.

Designed by Leonard Telesca

Library of Congress Cataloging in Publication Data

Patterson, Jerry E
    Antiques of sport

    Bibliography: p.
    Includes index.
    1.   Sporting goods—Collectors and collecting.
I.   Title.
GV745.P33   1975   796'.028   75-6569
ISBN 0-517-51876-7

Acknowledgments

The subject of this book was suggested by my editor, Kathryn Pinney, and I am grateful not only for her original suggestion, but for her continued assistance at every stage.

I also much appreciate the assistance of:

James F. Carr of New York City, who has kindly had photographed a large number of the interesting antiques of sport in his possession and permitted me to use them here. He has also allowed me to reproduce other illustrations from his extensive photographic archives.

Mr. and Mrs. Edward W. Sheldon of Mount Kisco, New York, who allowed me to illustrate a number of their fine trophies and to use their unpublished diary of African big game hunting.

Joan Hartley of Sotheby Parke Bernet Los Angeles who supplied some of the most interesting trophy photographs from sales held by Sotheby in Los Angeles.

For assistance and permission to publish photographs I am grateful to:

American Gallery of Sports Art, Inc., Dallas; Austrian Information Service, New York; Mrs. King Buckley, Keeneland Library, Lexington, Kentucky; J. David Garmaise, Canada Post, Ottawa; Miss Fiona Ford, Clark Nelson Ltd., London; Rupert Gentle, Milton Lilbourne, Wiltshire; German Information Center, New York; Graham Gallery, New York; Hennessy & Co., New York; Steve Henry, National Fresh Water Fishing Hall of Fame, Hayward, Wisconsin; D. Wayne Johnson, Medallic Art Co., Danbury, Conn.; Peter Johnson, Phillips Auctioneers, London; Mrs. Patricia Lowe, Will Rogers Memorial, Claremore, Okla.; Mrs. Elaine C. Mann, National Museum of Racing, Inc., Saratoga Springs, New York; Martini & Rossi, New York; Peter Morse, Honolulu; Michael A. Mosesson, Central Library, Walsall, England; Albert K. Baragwanath, Senior Curator, and Miss Charlotte La Rue, Museum of the City of New York; Mrs. Robert D. Nicoll, Mark Twain Memorial, Hartford; Dr. Dustan Osborn, Halifax, N. S.; William H. Ottley, National Pilots Association, Washington, D.C.; Howard J. Rabinowitz, The Gallery, Amsterdam, New York; Reed & Barton; Howard Ricketts, London; W. J. Schieffelin III, New York; Bill Schroeder, Citizens Savings Athletic Foundation, Los Angeles; Sotheby's Belgravia, London; Patrick A. Leavy, Tiffany & Co., New York; Craig E. Taylor, Lacrosse Hall of Fame Foundation, Baltimore; United States Parachute Association, Washington, D.C.; Jack H. van Praag, American Badminton Association; Victoria and Albert Museum, London; Otto Zenke, Greensboro, North Carolina; John Redding, National Baseball Hall of Fame and Museum, Inc., Cooperstown, New York; The National Football League, New York.

I am fortunate enough to have as my local reading room the New York Society Library, founded in 1754. The research for this book was mainly done at the Library and, like so many other New Yorkers of the last two centuries, I am continually grateful to the most helpful staff of that institution.

Contents

Introduction   ix

1. The Background of Today's Collecting   1

2. Antiques of the Horse Sports   33

3. Angling and Shooting Antiques   49

4. Game Trophies   73

5. Awards   93

6. Sports Memorabilia, Autographs, and Photographs   115

7. New Paths in Sports Collecting   137

Bibliography   144

Index   146

Introduction

Love of sports is one of the oldest of human traditions. The desire for exercise, especially outdoors, and recreation has kept sports at the forefront of daily life since time immemorial. The long tradition of engaging in a variety of sports is especially strong in the English-speaking world. The language itself is pervaded by sporting terms. Wherever English is spoken—Britain, America, Australia, New Zealand, South Africa, India—it is enriched with words and turns of speech, many of them extremely ancient, derived from hawking, hunting, shooting, angling, and—more recently—from cricket, baseball, and football.

The heritage of objects deriving from sports is also rich. No matter how simple their appearance and humble their origin, most of these objects are being collected today. Most sports, particularly those that became popular in the nineteenth century, require more or less elaborate equipment; in fact, the majority of the antiques of sport discussed here fall into the equipment category. It ranges from knives and guns to riding crops, hunting horns, and baseball bats. Not only very old sports like hawking have their collectible antiques; so do younger ones like football. In this book the majority of the antiques discussed derive from sports engaged in outdoors, with emphasis on hunting, shooting, fishing, and other sports of individual performance.

The book also describes the rewards of sport—the mounted heads, cups, medals, and other prizes given to winners in competitions, whether man against man or man against animal. Even sports that have little or no equipment to preserve have an array of trophies, badges, and medals for the enthusiast to collect.

The memorabilia of sports include objects that are relics of a famous player and the souvenirs that have been and are being produced to commemorate both sports and individual players. These souvenirs are very much a phenomenon of the twentieth century; the majority are not by any definition as yet antique, but they are being widely collected. Some of the most popular categories are discussed in this book.

Antiques of Sport also deals with two other branches of sports collecting. The first is sports autographs, a field that has not been entirely ignored by collectors, but has suffered for years from being regarded by adults as largely a juvenile hobby. Today it is emerging as a significant new area of serious autograph collecting. Sports photography is another area that is sharing a rapidly increasing new enthusiasm—the collecting of historic photographs; it is also dealt with here. The depiction of sports in paintings, prints, and sculptures is another subject, and an enormous one, and is not discussed here in depth.

One of the main purposes of this book is to tell the collector what kinds of objects, and from what period, are likely to be available in the many different categories. Fortunately, the supply of most antiques of sports, memorabilia, autographs, and photographs is large and shows few signs of drying up. So much fine sporting equipment, for example, was produced during the nineteenth century and continues to be made in this century that collectors have a reasonably good chance of finding worthwhile items. *All the prices mentioned in this book are actual sums realized at public sales or listed in dealers' catalogues or the specialized publications of the various sports.*

I

THE BACKGROUND OF TODAY'S COLLECTING

Collectors in any field of antiques want to know what material is likely to be available to collect. Antiques of sport have their own special attraction and like every field of collecting their own special set of limitations. Some sports have always required so much equipment that antique objects survive in great quantity. From other sports, little remains for the collector.

The quantity of equipment, trophies, and memorabilia of a particular sport to be found on the collectors' market of the present day is not necessarily in proportion to the recorded history of that sport. A long history by no means guarantees the preservation of numerous antiques. The equipment of the sport may have been minimal to begin with, or too fragile to preserve or impossible to identify today—the various sports using balls are examples. The composition of the ball is not often very lasting (bowling balls are an exception), and before the standardization of the various ball games in the late nineteenth century one ball might be used in several sports.

There are sports with no equipment at all —swimming is one. Its only antiques are awards. Very ancient sports like most track and field events, which were part of the classical Olympics and have a known history of nearly three thousand years, have never required much, if any, equipment. Not even special apparel was necessary at the Olympics, since the athletes appeared naked. The sport of walking (sometimes called race-walking) was extremely popular in the seventies of the last century, and 100-mile walks drew large crowds of spectators. One J. B. Gillie was the first American athlete to walk 100 miles in less than twenty-four hours. The current record is sixteen hours and fifty-five minutes, and walking is an Olympic sport. Obviously, it is a sport with few antiques.

Generally speaking, sports of individual achievement produce many more antiques for the collector than do team sports. Hunting and fishing and sports involving animals, especially the horse, are good examples from both the past and the present of sports requiring considerable equipment. In the twentieth century, however, team sports like baseball and football have inspired quantities of made-to-order souvenirs, trophies, and memorabilia.

Every antique collector is by definition a student of history. The history of sports is particularly interesting; not many chapters in human history tell more about the way people actually lived in the past. Few sports, however, have a precisely known beginning. It is a measure of the importance of recreation in human life that most of the sports popular today grew so naturally and slowly out of the daily existence of times past no one can say exactly when they began or, in many cases, where. Hunting, shooting, and fishing obviously had their origins in the quest for food, but their practice, even as recreation, is immemorially old. Only their equipment has changed, as will be shown.

Some sports developed in various parts of the world at different times. Others spread from their home country into new countries, where they were adopted and modified. Polo is an example of such a game. Its origin was in Persia, but it has a history, too, in India, Tibet, China, and Japan. Collectors of ceramics will immediately think of the pottery figures of polo players recovered from Chinese tombs of the seventh to ninth

centuries A.D. The game now is associated with India, where it was revived in the nineteenth century; with England, where it was introduced by British army officers in 1869, and with the United States, where James Gordon Bennett, publisher of the *New York Herald*, brought it in 1876. Such a diffuse history is typical of many sports.

Only slowly have most sports acquired rules, organization, and sophistication. The majority of the team sports widely played today evolved gradually from simple rustic amusements. Kicking, throwing, or hitting an object around—or knocking it down on the village green—led in time to football, soccer, hockey, rugby, bowling, and similar games. The development was slow. Although primitive forms of these games date back at least to the Middle Ages, their rules were not standardized until the nineteenth century when they moved off the village green onto school playing fields and then into professional stadiums. The Wimbledon Hockey Club standardized that game in 1883. The Rugby Football Union was formed in 1871. The London Soccer Association organized in 1863. And the rules for American football were drawn up in 1873 by representatives of Columbia, Princeton, Rutgers, and Yale colleges. Bowling was standardized as a ten-pin game in 1895.

Some sports have a somewhat more specific origin. Croquet is said to have been introduced into England by an Irish lady, a Miss MacNaughton, in the year 1862, when it was first played under her tutelage, but it probably had been played in eighteenth-century Ireland and is possibly even older. The 1862 occasion, however, launched the game into immense popularity in England and America. Few games have ever been taken up so quickly and so ardently. The first American organization was the Park Place Croquet Club of Brooklyn, organized as early as 1864. From the beginning the game was played by both sexes and, indeed, speedily became *the* sport to combine with flirtation. For years it was called "the court-

Catching fish and wildfowl with a net was both necessity and sport in the ancient world. Netting is shown in this scene, which is more than thirty-eight centuries old. On an Egyptian wall painting of the XIIth dynasty (circa 2000 B.C.) is depicted a good catch of wild ducks and geese by the seated man. Courtesy of Metropolitan Museum of Art, New York

Polo is a very ancient game that reached the United States in the last third of the nineteenth century. The international matches between British and American teams were first played in 1886. In its early days polo was played on fields near racetracks, immediately after the races. In 1896 the photographer Byron caught this scene at a polo match at Prospect Park, Brooklyn. The Byron Collection, Museum of the City of New York

The most famous date in the history of football is 6 November 1869. Rutgers and Princeton played each other that day at New Brunswick, New Jersey, in the first intercollegiate game. The field was quite crowded—there were twenty-five players on each side—and the game quite different from today's, as the players were not allowed to run with the ball. In 1969, the Chevrolet Company commissioned a series of paintings by Arnold Friberg honoring the centennial of college football. The famous Rutgers-Princeton meeting is shown here. Medallic Art Company, Danbury, Conn.

The official college football centennial medal was designed by Justin Fairbanks and struck in bronze in 1969. Medallic Art Company, Danbury, Conn.

ing game." A tougher, all-male variety called roque was developed, but croquet maintained its popularity for decades. No game is more associated with the Victorian era.

Even recently developed sports like baseball have origins that are the subject of vigorous dispute among their followers. The place and date of baseball's origin and the identity of the founding father have been quite controversial questions. General Abner Doubleday and Alexander J. Cartwright are usually mentioned as founders; each has had his supporters among historians and fans of the game. A National Baseball Commission in 1908, by official decree, gave General Doubleday "title to the distinction of having originated the game of baseball." The year of origin was declared to be 1839 and the place where the game was first played, Cooperstown, New York. When the centennial came around in 1939, the National Baseball Hall of Fame and Museum was dedicated at Cooperstown and a United States stamp issued to commemorate the

first hundred years of the game. The question of the founder was still so controversial, however, that it was decided the game rather than any individual should be honored on the stamp. The design includes the diamond-shaped playing field said to have been laid out by Doubleday at Cooperstown in the summer of 1839.

Rarely has a sport actually been invented. The most famous example is undoubtedly basketball, which was invented in the United States in 1891 by James A. Naismith, physical education teacher at the YMCA College in Springfield, Massachusetts.

Fashion is extremely pronounced in the history of sports. Whereas the popularity of a few, like hunting, remains fixed, others have had a curious up-and-down sequence of activity. Track and field athletics (principally running, jumping, and throwing) were the basis of the ancient Olympic games and also popular in the Roman era, but they were in a comatose condition for centuries. The first college meet was not held until

An unusual antique of the sport of archery, as practiced in the ancient Far East, is the archer's ring. Such a ring was worn on the thumb, which in China was cocked around the bowstring when that was pulled back; in the European method, two fingers are cocked around the string. Peter Morse of Honolulu, a collector and authority on archer rings, says: "Since the eighteenth century, the rings have been used less for sport and more for the personal adornment of males. They apparently had and still have some implications of scholarly attainments, and are no more functional in their original sense than are Phi Beta Kappa keys as keys." The rings have been made of jade, porcelain, wood, Peking glass, cloisonné, cinnabar, Venetian glass, and semiprecious stones. The ancient Mogul style, shown in this example, was wood with gold and silver inlays. Peter Morse, Honolulu

1864, when Oxford met Cambridge. Now track and field are again major events in the revived Olympics.

Roller skating has had a curious history. It was introduced as a sport, then called "wheel skating," about 1844 at the London Coliseum. The skating was done on a wooden floor. Its popularity was intense but short-lived. About thirty years later improved skates with ball bearings brought a second vogue and the building of rinks. Roller skating became the rage in the United States, where a team sport called "roller polo" resembling ice hockey was invented and drew large crowds of spectators in the 1880s and '90s. It was even played professionally. Now roller skating, although no longer that popular, has its tournaments and championships for men and women.

Archery also has had more than one dramatic, if brief, revival. The use of the bow and arrow is prehistoric, very likely dating back to the Paleolithic Age. In the Far East, the use of archer rings is very ancient. In the late Middle Ages, the bow and arrow was the principal European weapon for tak-

ing game and was used as well in war. Firearms had effectively superseded it for both purposes by the sixteenth century. Archery was first revived in England as a target sport by King Charles II after his restoration to the throne in 1660. Hitting the bull's-eye amused the court. That fashion passed, but beginning in the 1860s archery or "toxophily" ("love of the bow," a manufactured word used after about 1800) underwent an amazing revival. It became a great pastime for women, then rather restricted in their choice of sports. In the 1880s in England "archeresses," dressed in the full fig of the day, puffed sleeves and all, practiced with their bows and arrows. Societies were formed with names like "The Bow-Women of the Wye." In the United States the sport also caught on in the 1880s.

Sports have a way of changing from a necessity into a recreation. Hunting and fishing are the natural examples, but there are others—the sport of coaching or "four-in-hand driving," for example. Coach driving was taken up by amateurs only after the coming of the railroads had made travel by

Antique Chinese archer's ring (center) *with jade case* (left) *and brass button. The ensemble was worn as a belt ornament and attached to the belt by the cords shown.* Peter Morse, Honolulu

Nineteenth-century Chinese archer's ring carved of jade with a motif of two horses. In general, the rings sought by collectors are carved jade. Peter Morse, Honolulu

Porcelain Chinese archer's ring of the nineteenth century. Peter Morse, Honolulu

coach no longer a necessity but quite the reverse—a luxury, and an unusually costly one at that. In addition, in the days just before the railroad vanquished the coach, the technical improvements in vehicles made amateur driving safer and more comfortable. Roads began to be macadamized, and therefore became much smoother in the 1820s. Until about 1815, the coachman's seat had been superimposed independently on the forecarriage; it was springless, and the amount of jarring the driver endured on unpaved roads can be imagined. After that time, the seat became part of the body, had springs, and was much more comfortable. The public was not happy with this change. They did not want the coachman to be comfortable; he might go to sleep and wreck them. Passengers liked the idea of his being shaken and jolted into wakefulness.

The sport of driving coaches for pleasure was introduced in the 1860s and taken up by the richest sportsmen in England and America—the Duke of Beaufort in England, for example, and in the United States the Vanderbilts, Havemeyers, Iselins, and Schermerhorns. Enormous sums were spent on horses, carriages, and liveries to get a spanking "turnout." Again in the 1970s, coaching was revived in Great Britain, where it has been patronized by Prince Philip, who himself drives. Still an expensive sport, it is estimated in the '70s that the harness set alone for a four-in-hand costs over $5,000.

In the last few years bicycling, a sport nearly one hundred years old, has undergone one of these remarkable revivals. Riding the bicycle for fun and competition assumed major dimensions in Europe and the United States in the 1880s and '90s. The

In the days when cycling flourished as a sport it had its own trophies. In September 1891, G. Bow won this shield-shaped cycling trophy given by the South West Ham Rovers Cycling Club to the victor in its five-mile challenge race. The trophy was made in Birmingham in 1889. In 1972, is was sold at auction in London for $125. Sotheby's Belgravia, London

Opposite page

The usual male costume for bicycling, as shown in this photograph of William M. Pinney, an ardent cyclist of the 1890s, was knickers with high socks. If trousers were worn they were clipped around the leg tightly so they would not get entangled in the spokes of the wheels.

The bicycling craze of the late nineteenth century produced all sorts of odd two-wheeled vehicles and even a few with three or four wheels. One of the most famous types is the "ordinary" with grotesquely disproportionate wheels. Mark Twain owned this one. Mark Twain Memorial, Hartford, Conn.

C. E. Churchill,　MAIN STREET,　Arcade, N. Y.

League of American Wheelmen, which was organized in 1880, held races and agitated for good roads on which to pursue their sport. Although the bicycle in various primitive forms had a history stretching back to the eighteenth century, it was not really practicable until mid-nineteenth century. Interestingly, one of the first practical two-wheeled vehicles driven by pedals was originated by Baron Karl Drais von Sauerbronn, chief forester of the Grand Duchy of Baden in Germany, who used the simple contrivance on his tours of the grand ducal forests to check the timber and game preserved there. Not until the invention of the "safety"

bicycle with wheels of approximately equal size in the 1880s did the sport become widespread.

Long cross-country bicycle rides were the rage in the United States and participated in by both sexes. The clubs, generally called "Wheelmen" with some geographical adjective (typical in New York were "The Gramercy and Metropolist Wheelmen," "The Windsor Terrace Wheelmen," and "The Kings County Wheelmen"), organized rides called "runs" of up to one hundred miles (a "century run") as a single-day outing. The average pace was eight to ten miles per hour. A typical run was a "century" from Fifty-ninth Street, Manhattan, to White Plains and return on 27 October 1895. The wheelmen and women left at 5:00 A.M., had breakfast in Larchmont, dinner in White Plains, and arrived back at Fifty-ninth Street at 6:30 P.M.

The coming of the automobile sent this sport into decline for many years, although demand by children and some adults for bicycles kept the production at around a million a year during the 1930s. In 1947, the annual sales of bicycles amounted to about two million. In the early 1970s, however, bicycling was revived for both transport and recreation, and production perked up. In 1971, sales were nearly nine million, in 1972 nearly fourteen million, and in 1973 more than fifteen million. At the same time there was great interest in the history of the sport and in its antiques. Old bicycles of various vintages and stages of development came on the collectors' market, first in flea markets, then into the important auctions.

Most of the sports mentioned, especially when new, were first engaged in by rich or at least well-to-do people. Sports that have left collectible antiques have been associated with people of means. As necessary activities have developed into sports, they have been enjoyed by people who had the leisure to participate and the wherewithal to afford nongainful activities and the required equipment. Many, probably most, of the articles mentioned throughout this book were, when they were first produced, luxurious and expensive things that could be acquired only through a fairly substantial expenditure of money.

Sports connected with animals, especially, have a closeness with wealth in European civilization. Traditionally, many rich people have had both affection for domestic animals and the desire, and means, to slay wild animals. The association is based on the fact that only the rich have had the means to breed nonproductive animals and keep them to be killed at leisure. Formerly,

in fact, most animals were the property of the upper classes. The horses of the Middle Ages were primarily used as mounts by the knightly class. Deer, foxes, and hares as well as most birds and fish were preserved as game animals for killing by the lord at his will and for his recreation. Laws against poaching game—that is, taking it without permission—were frightfully severe and remained so for centuries. In enlightened eighteenth-century England a law was in effect that forbade people having an income of less than one hundred pounds a year (then quite a high figure) to kill game at all—even on their own land. In other words, the very great majority of people, freeholders included, were prevented by the Game Acts from killing their own animals, so to speak, even for eating. They had to be preserved as "game" for killing by the sportsmen who had that privilege. Certain birds, in particular grouse and blackcock, were declared by statute to be "game," and it was forbidden to burn the heather and bracken where they hid except at stated times of the year. Such laws prevailed all over Europe, too.

In the United States poaching laws were never so widespread or so rigorous; the superabundance of game and the scarcity of people meant that there was little need for them. In the twentieth century, of course, nations all over the world have imposed a whole series of regulations on the sports of hunting and shooting. In many places the fines are quite heavy and prison terms are given for poaching. There are, in addition, many local licensing and limiting laws passed by local governments. Legal regulation is just as much with the sportsman as ever, only its structure is no longer based on class or rank.

The game preserved in Europe consisted not only of animals indigenous to Western Europe that were killed for sport, such as the stag and the hare, but in addition all sorts of exotic wildlife imported for pleasure

Europeans were fascinated by exotic animals from the Dark Ages on. Numerous medieval bestiaries testify to their longing for information about unusual fauna. Royalty and nobility imported strange animals and birds for their private menageries. This unsigned painting, probably Central European in origin and of the late seventeenth century, depicts Turks hunting the ostrich. Note the crescent on the turban at right. Although the horsemen are armed with spears, the object is probably to take the ostrich alive, as the birds were prized denizens of zoos and their feathers greatly desired for human adornment. Oil on canvas, 11¼ x 14¼ inches. Collection of James F. Carr, New York

The arms and armor for war and sport belonging to the Hapsburg family is the largest and best-documented collection in the world. Now preserved in the Hofburg Palace in Vienna, it includes the Hofjagdkammer *(Imperial Hunting Collection). The Galerie Franz Ferdinand, shown here, is named after the heir to the Austrian throne whose assassination in 1914 brought on the First World War. He was one of the most famous sportsmen of his time. The paintings are of hunting scenes; note also the fine stag's antlers.* Austrian Information Service, New York

and show from Roman times onward. The attitude toward them was always ambivalent. They were preserved, even petted, but certain species at least were pursued and killed for pleasure. The birds and animals that were not hunted have an amusing history. Parrots, for example, which had come into the royal menageries of Europe by the sixteenth century, were traditionally pets of the highborn. Those in the Hapsburg imperial zoo in Vienna were especially famous and especially pampered. In the time of the Empress Maria Theresa in the eighteenth century, a thousand gallons of fine Tokay wine were used each year just to soften the bread fed to the imperial birds.

In the early years of the nineteenth century the English royal Duchess of York kept a huge menagerie, which included parrots, at her palace outside London. At her death some of these birds were left as legacies to friends. At the same period parrots used to be sold at auction in London. One catalogue describing a gray parrot mentioned that he was "a matchless talker and does not know any bad language." The Duchess of York also kept kangaroos and ostriches. Rare animals and birds like these were never hunted, of course, but unusual animals like the aurochs (the European bison) and game birds like the capercailzie (a grouse the size of a small turkey) were carefully protected from poaching by the lower orders so they could be hunted at the proper season by the upper.

The involvement of the noble and rich with animals bordered on zoophilia. In England, the history of several generations of the Stanley family, earls of Derby, in the nineteenth century shows the interesting dichotomy of attitude toward animals. In 1824, the twelfth earl of Derby was considered a great patron of the art of cockfighting, then a popular sport with the young nobility; "the first and most spirited cocker of modern times," he was called. One of the richest men in England, Derby owned more than three thousand fighting cocks and kept a staff of expert feeders and "setters" to train them (the setter is the man who places the birds beak to beak at the beginning of the fight).

His son, the thirteenth earl, however, was devoted all his life to the preservation and study of rare animals and birds. He was president of the Zoological Society and had an African crane, among other wildlife, named after him. At Knowsley Park near Liverpool he developed a most extraordinary private menagerie. Estimates by his contemporaries as to what its maintenance cost him vary, but the expenses were said to run ten to fifteen thousand pounds annually. It is difficult to translate that into modern purchasing power—it was probably not less than $100,000 a year. The expenditure continued for many years. When the earl died in 1851, the diarist Henry Greville wrote: "He had a very extraordinary collection of birds and some other animals which will now be disposed of as the present Lord Derby does not inherit his father's taste in these matters." Greville's more sarcastic brother Charles summed up the earl in *his* diary by remarking that "he spent half a million in kangaroos." The fourteenth earl of Derby sold his father's menagerie and aviary at auction, in 1851. The most expensive mammals were the elands. Two gnus sold for nearly £300. Sales of live animals were not unusual then, giving the editors of the satiric weekly *Punch* the chance to ask how the auctioneer intended to "knock down" an elephant, to suggest that a tiger might "advance" on the audience rather than the bid receiving an advance, and to imply that a lot of monkeys might be "going, going, gone" before they were sold.

The fourteenth earl, although a busy statesman, loved hunting and shooting so much that he liked to say he "had been too busy with pheasants to attend to politics," a disturbing remark from a man who was colonial secretary and three times prime minister of Great Britain. Racing was another of his favorite sports. One of his biographers remarks severely: "His lordship's ready indulgence in sporting slang, even on the gravest occasions, occasioned some misgivings to his respectable middle-class supporters." The sixteenth earl, when governorgeneral of Canada in 1893, first presented the trophy called the Stanley Cup, which is still hockey's most coveted award.

The association of royalty and nobility with hunting, always the most popular sport with them, is clearly shown by the authorship of many volumes of what would now be called "how-to books" on the sport. One of the most famous of these is the *Livre de la Chasse*, written by Gaston Comte de Foix, who was nicknamed "Phoebus" on account of his yellow hair. He was born in 1331 and died in 1391—in a hunting accident. His book, which describes all manner of hunting as practiced in the fourteenth century, was partly translated into English as *The Master of Game* by another man of royal birth, Prince Edward of England, second Duke of York. Princes did not disdain to write treatises on other sports, especially on the royal sport of hawking. The Holy Roman Emperor Frederick II, who was born in 1194 and died in 1254 and was considered the greatest falconer of the Middle Ages, was the author of such a treatise. Another medieval monarch, John the Good of France, who lived in the fourteenth century, had an introduction to the art of hawking written in verse for his young son. A glance at nearly any medieval illuminated manuscript or any tapestry collection will show the importance of hunting (with bow and arrow or spear) and hawking in the life of the nobility of the Middle Ages. The celebrated series of tapestries known as "The Unicorn" at New York's Metropolitan Museum of Art are a virtual encyclopedia of the hunt as it was practiced about 1500.

In medieval times the stag was hunted "by force of hounds," meaning pursued with dogs while the hunters were mounted or even on foot. This is the style of hunt usually shown on the tapestries. The method, which was of course very hard work for the hunters, had been substantially abandoned by the sixteenth century. The battue then became the usual method of taking game in many countries. The royal courts arranged drives in which vast numbers of beaters (servants, gamekeepers, and peasants) drove (i.e. "beat up") the game (mainly stags, boars, foxes, hares) into an ambush, where the lord and his party were waiting to make the kill. These drives made possible an extraordinary slaughter of animals. Two successive sixteenth-century electors of Saxony recorded a total between them of 110,530 deer, 54,200 wild boar, and innumerable smaller game killed on their battues.

The pleasure of the chase or battue was a passion with royalty from the most ancient times. Monarchs almost without exception, it seems, were devoted to hunting stag and shooting pheasant. Some appear to have been absorbed in the sport to the exclusion of statecraft. When Louis XV did *not* go hunting, his courtiers said quite seriously: "The king does nothing today." His cousin Charles, king of Naples, issued royal orders —absurd but deadly serious—to protect the game on his preserves, the penalty for anyone killing or even molesting pheasants or rabbits on his island of Procida being seven years in the galleys! No dogs or cats could be kept near a royal preserve, and pheasant feathers found in a private house were evidence strong enough to place the householder under torture.

The importance of hunting was reflected in painting and all the decorative arts, including even porcelain: The Meissen factory made porcelain figures showing bison, wolf,

Opposite page

Everyone is familiar with the depiction of sports in innumerable paintings and prints, but sporting themes have also attracted artists in ceramics. Many nineteenth-century Staffordshire pottery figures, designed as chimney ornaments, portrayed sportsmen. The pair pictured are cricketers, a bowler at left and a batsman at right, approximately 14 inches high. They were sold at auction in 1973 for $1,100. Other sports of which English pottery figures are known include archery, prizefighting, horse racing, and bullbaiting. Phillips Auctioneers, London

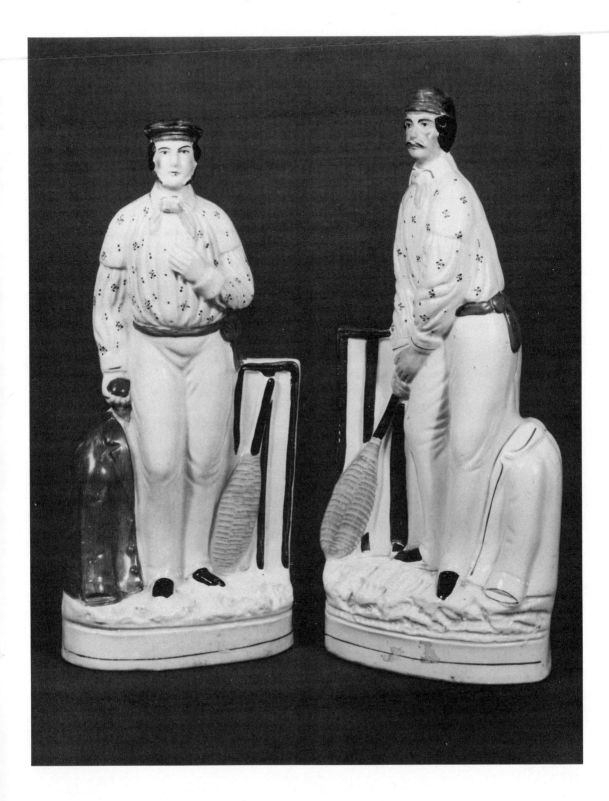

boar, bear, and stag hunts from the early days of its production in the 1740s. The Elector Augustus III of Saxony, who established Meissen, even ordered a dish cover (*Jagddeckel*) ornamented with figures of huntsmen surrounded by dogs and quarry, which he used at the electoral hunting lodge at Hubertusburg. Similar pieces were made at many manufactories of porcelain and pottery.

Even more than hunting, hawking was a princely and kingly sport. Its devotees have proudly called falconry "the oldest sport known to man." It is one of the best examples of an ancient sport still practiced today. Its history is amply documented in books and art, and it has provided the language with a still-living vocabulary. Falconry was known in Western Europe before the Crusades in the eleventh century, but the Crusaders brought back many new techniques from the Near East, where the sport had already flourished for centuries and where it is pursued today. Royal decrees relating to falconry go back at least to the days of the Emperor Charlemagne in the ninth century. Very harsh sentences were given to those who stole valuable birds. Later in the Middle Ages, the nobility carried their favorite hawks everywhere with them on their wrists, even to church, and trained falcons were often given as part payment of feudal dues. On occasion, the clergy were known to accept them as religious tithes. The falcons given in payment of dues and tithes were already trained—a tedious and time-consuming process—and fitted with chain, bell, and the hood that is used to cover the bird's eyes and removed only when actually hunting. Ownership of falcons was, surprisingly, not restricted to the nobility and clergy. The celebrated *Boke of Saint Albans* (1486), the earliest English printed book on sport, gives a list of kinds of falcons and hawks appropriate for each rank of medieval society.

Hawking was always a sport in which women participated. The illuminated manuscripts and tapestries of the Middle Ages make this clear. Women preferred the gentler sport of falconry to the rougher forms of hunting. Merlins, which are small and elegantly shaped birds, were especially favored by ladies.

The hawks were held on the fist of the sportsman and sportswoman by "jesses," two strips of soft leather, one end attached to each leg, the other end held in the falconer's hand. A bell was also attached to each leg of the bird to help in locating her after she had flown at her game and was out of the falconer's sight. According to the charming dictum of the *Boke of Saint Albans*, the bells should be of equal weight but not make exactly the same sound; one should be a semitone under the other. This equipment, examples of which survive as probably the earliest Western European antiques of sport, with little change is used today by falconers.

The most exact and complex vocabulary existed in all European languages for the bird and the sport. Each claw of the bird and even each feather had its particular name. Unsurpassed for elegance, hawking terms have contributed many expressions to current English. A hawk was "disclosed," not "hatched." An "eyas" was a young hawk taken from the nest ("eyrie"); a "haggard," an adult hawk that had learned to hunt (or "prey") before she was captured. A hawk was a "brancher" when she had learned to fly from branch to branch. She "rejoiced" when she sharpened her beak and shook her feathers after catching game.

The equipment of hawking, too, has provided the language with some apt and amusing expressions. A "cadge" is the wooden frame on which the hawks are perched and transported to and from the hunting field. The men who carried them, "cadgers," did no real work, but they received tips from those who came to watch the sport. Hence, a "cadger" is a fellow out to get something for nothing. A bird that is molting is said to be "intermewing"; hence, the place where she is kept is "The Mews," a word still in use for back street housing,

Falconry, the sport of kings and nobles for a thousand years, has had equipment made for it from the finest materials. These two magnificent bags for holding game brought down by the falcons are made of pink and blue silk with gold threads and engraved brass mounts. They are believed to have been made around 1630 for an Austrian archduke. Austrian Information Service, New York

often converted stables in the larger cities.

The practice of falconry declined everywhere by the seventeenth century. Louis XIII of France, who reigned from 1610 to 1643 and was an almost maniacally intent sportsman, was one of the last great patrons of the art. Falconry had a revival beginning in the 1930s and has its devotees today in America and Europe. It has never been eclipsed in the Near East and flourishes there in all its ancient style, actively practiced by rich sportsmen throughout the region. It is claimed that the emirate of Kuwait produces the modern world's best falcon trainers, and that there were in 1973 more than two thousand trained falcons in the small country. The falcons, which can cost several thousand dollars each, are mainly used to hunt the *hubara* bird (a bustard). The Kuwait coat of arms displays a falcon.

Hunting and hawking were the sports of the gentry, but humble people engaged in sports that involved less expenditure, less equipment, and generally less time. Swimming was one such sport, the various ball games mentioned earlier, and trials of strength—boxing and wrestling. Swimming, now one of the newsmaking sports and a great attention-getter at the Olympics, was

not an organized sport until the late nineteenth century. The English Channel was
first successfully swum by Matthew Webb
in 1875. Boxing and wrestling, very popular,
especially among rustics, in eighteenth-century England and on the nineteenth-century
American frontier, also had to wait until the
final third of the last century to become
sports with rules and standards.

The expression "rude sports" used in
seventeenth- and eighteenth-century literature was only too descriptive of some village
pastimes. One of the most dreadful was
bullbaiting, in which dogs were set on a
bull. The bull was generally "worried"
rather than killed outright, but both bull
and dogs were injured. This attraction was
popular in England between the seventeenth and nineteenth centuries. The traveling bull was then an institution. He was led
from village to village and at each new spot
was tethered to a stake. A hole was dug in
the ground of a size sufficient for the bull to
cover his muzzle, that being the spot on
which trained dogs were taught to lay hold.
After paying a small fee, "bull hankers"
might then set their dogs at the animal. It
was always a sport of low repute and always
abhorred by a large segment of the population. During the era of reform in England
bullbaiting, bull running (in which the bull
was run down and killed by men), bearbaiting (setting dogs on a chained bear), and
dogfighting were all prohibited by an act of
Parliament.

With regard to cockfighting, it is only
fair to say that before the mid-nineteenth
century few people found the sport outraged
their humane feelings. Many followers of
racing, hunting, and the other horse sports
also enjoyed cockfighting. The American
sporting writer F. Gray Griswold, writing of
nineteenth-century sport in the United
States and Europe, said firmly: "I believe
that gamecocks are intended to fight just
as I believe that canary birds are created to
sing." Nevertheless cockfighting became
illegal in England in 1849 and gradually was

outlawed in most parts of the United States.

In the American colonial settlements a
distasteful sport was "riding the goose"
(also called "plucking" or "pulling the
goose"). This consisted of smearing the
neck and head of a goose with oil or soap
and fastening it by a rope, neck down, high
up between two poles. Mounted contestants
rode at full gallop and attempted to seize
the goose, usually breaking its neck but not
immediately killing it. It is somewhat reas-
suring to know that in 1654 the cranky
Peter Stuyvesant, Director General of New
Amsterdam, absolutely forbade the practice
of "riding the goose." Attempts have been
made periodically to revive it, one in South
Carolina as recently as 1947. And in parts
of the world such cruel sports survive with
considerable popularity: cockfighting, which
is a national sport in the Philippines and
popular in the southern United States, dogfighting in the midwestern United States,
bullfighting in Spain and other countries.

Fortunately, the antique collector can
ignore these sports, as they have left little
equipment to collect with the exception of
the bullfighter's dress and swords and the
spurs for gamecocks, although in the fields
of painting, prints, and books they have been
frequently depicted.

The dates and places enumerated for the
organization of various sports show that by
far the largest number of these are played
today under rules developed in the British
Isles. The United States lacks a long history
in many sports, for the obvious reason of its
comparatively late settlement. The great
expenditure in time and money necessary
for sports like staghunting and hawking was
simply beyond the capability of the sparsely
settled United States before well into the
nineteenth century.

Reading the decrees passed by the gov-
ernors of the Dutch West India Company
settlement at New Amsterdam indicates
that the usual colonial sports were boating,
fishing, skating, fowling (taking birds with
a net or gun), bowling, "shovelboard," tur-

key shooting, and golf (played with a "small ball, a crooked club, and a series of small holes in the turf"). Elsewhere in the colonies, racing fast horses, a sport regarded as typically American by Europeans, got an early hold on people's attention that has never diminished. In general, however, the United States entered the nineteenth century with most of its sports in their infancy compared to their development in Britain and on the continent.

In the nineteenth century a few older sports declined, others were revived, and many new ones appeared. Mountaineering, for example, began to attract worldwide attention. Before the late eighteenth century the sensation mountains had inspired in most people was mainly dread, and they were ignored by sportsmen except for occasional hunting on their lower reaches. Mont Blanc in the Alps was first climbed in 1786 and some other Alpine peaks were ascended between 1800 and 1850. The Alpine Club of London was founded in 1858. But the landmark date in the history of mountain climbing is the ascent of the Matterhorn (summit 14,701), which was first scaled in 1865 by the Englishman Edward Whymper and his party, four of whom fell to their deaths on the descent. This was Whymper's sixth attempt on the peak. It is a curiosity of the history of many sports of individual performance that once a barrier of time or distance is broken, the way seems to be open to all comers. After Whymper's success the Matterhorn was climbed, and continues to be climbed, by thousands. In the summer of 1974 the Zermatt Tourist Bureau reported that an average of 150 climbers reached the summit every day. The top, which is fifty yards long, can hold only about forty people at a time, and so guides keep orderly lines of climbers waiting their turn at it.

The class with the leisure to indulge in sport was much larger by the middle of the nineteenth century—and, on the whole,

richer—and there was a great increase in the hours devoted to sport of all kind. Sportsmen who clung to the ways of simpler days were astonished and dismayed by the changes. "Formerly," wrote Robert Surtees, author of hunting novels and editor of the *New Sporting Magazine*, in the 1830s, "hunting, with shooting, satisfied a man. A little hunting might be done from home and a little shooting, both in reason and moderation. But now everybody must do everything: hunt in Leicestershire, shoot in Scotland, fish in Norway, race at Newmarket, and yacht everywhere."

Perhaps the best-known sporting writer of nineteenth-century England was Charles James Apperley, who wrote innumerable sporting books and articles under the name "Nimrod." His attitude is interesting: to him fox hunting was the supreme sport. During his career he hunted with no less than eighty-two packs of foxhounds, besides making numerous runs with staghounds and harriers. Nimrod had a marked distaste for sports that involved a large number of people and sports he considered "dirty." He hated cockfighting, for instance, although it was an immensely popular sport in his time, trapshooting with live pigeons, and bullbaiting. He enjoyed shooting over dogs but hated the increasing crowd of keepers and beaters who served the sport; large bags meant nothing to him. "Pheasants and hares in abundance were of course slaughtered on this afternoon," he wrote of one day's shooting, "but don't let us call it sporting."

Interestingly enough, he detested a sport that was new in the 1830s, now thought of as quintessentially English—steeplechasing—because so many horses were injured during the race in those days. He called it flatly "cruel and unsportsmanlike." In 1840, he wrote: "a disgusting exhibition of this nature, absurdly designated the Grand National Steeple Chase, has just taken place. Eight horses out of thirteen fell."

When Surtees founded the *New Sporting*

Magazine in 1832, he firmly excluded from it all mention of bullbaiting, cockfighting, and boxing "as low and demoralising pursuits." The periodical emphasized the horse sports, particularly hunting (Surtees was the author of one of the most famous hunting novels, *Jorrocks' Jaunts and Jollities*) and racing.

The late eighteenth century and the early nineteenth were the era of the eccentric English sportsman. The celebrated John Mytton, for example, who on his sporting days avoided as frequently as possible the horrors of sobriety. He once deliberately rode over a course riddled with rabbit holes; naturally, his horse fell and, what was worse, rolled over on him. But he survived that and many other sporting mishaps, even the hazard of duck hunting stark naked in the English climate. Another mildly demented sportsman was the "Mad Earl" of Orford, who insisted on harnessing stags to his coach and driving them four-in-hand until one day his team was set upon by a pack of passing buckhounds and bolted, smashing the rig and very nearly the earl. Or the amiable John Peel, of Troutbeck, who hunted with a pack of foxhounds for fifty-five years. When he died in 1854, his family had the headstone of his grave ornamented with emblems of the hunt. He is the hero of the famous song that starts

D'ye ken John Peel with his coat so gay?
D'ye John Peel at the break of day?
D'ye ken John Peel when he's far far away
With his hounds and his horn in the
    morning?

Before the First World War the amount of time and energy expended on sports by the royalty, nobility, and upper classes of Europe and the British Isles, and to a lesser extent the American rich, was quite unbelievable. In fact, some did little else. "There are people," remarked one critic, "of the highest rank in the England of today, whose existence is as much nomadic as that of Red Indians in the reserve territories of North America . . . they migrate from one hunting ground to another as the diminution of game impels them."

The preservation of game remained all-important to sportsmen, with consequent irritation of farmers on whose land it grazed. One writer said young men of the upper classes in England were brought up like young gamekeepers and seemed to regard the historic mansions they inhabited as "merely comfortable preserves for different kinds of game." Poaching was still regarded, as in medieval times, as a heinous offense. Man-traps with iron jaws as cruel as those used by poachers to capture edible animals were set out by landlords to catch poachers. The main era for the manufacture of these mechanisms in England was about 1800. Collections of man-traps have been formed, incredibly enough, in modern times. In 1971 a collection of sixteen was sold at auction in England to a museum for a total of $1,600.

The sports program at the famous Ranelagh Club in London gives an idea of the range of athletic pastimes available during the Victorian and Edwardian ages. Ranelagh was (and is) primarily a polo club, where famous matches were played, but its fields were host to many other sports events. The first balloon race started at Ranelagh and the first airship was also launched (it failed to rise and eventually floated away like a cigar-shaped balloon). The first bicycle gymkhana took place there in the presence of Queen Alexandra, who distributed the prizes. (The word *gymkhana*, originally an Anglo-Indian expression for any sports display, came into great fashion during the second half of the nineteenth century.) At Ranelagh in the first motor gymkhana the Hon. Charles Rolls took several prizes with an automobile shaped and made like a horse-drawn wagonette, ancestor of the famous car he was to make with F. H. Royce. There were many meets of sports in vogue like coaching, archery, lawn tennis, and croquet.

The social impetus for sport in England came straight from the top. King Edward VII, both as Prince of Wales and King, was a passionate sportsman. Despite a girth of forty-eight inches (behind his broad back he was referred to as "Tum-Tum"), he played lawn tennis and croquet, fenced, hunted, and, above all, shot. Fishing he disliked because it is largely a solitary sport, and he could not bear to be alone, but he shot all his life. As a young man of nineteen in 1860 when he visited the United States, he was taken to the outskirts of Chicago, then not very far from the center of town, to shoot prairie fowl, quail, plover, and a few cranes.

The Sandringham estate was the king's own sporting establishment and was devoted primarily to shooting. Situated on the flatlands of Norfolk, it was ideal for guns. During Edward's lifetime the total head of game killed annually there rose from 7,000 to 30,000, but he also rented neighboring shoots and went abroad for game. During his trips to Egypt he shot crocodiles (his first was a female nine feet long), cormorants, cranes, doves, flamingos, hawk owls, herons, hoopoes, mallards, merlins, and spoonbills. In Sweden he shot elk. On a royal trip to that country, four hundred beaters served forty-six guns stretched over a long distance, and on one day fifty-two elk, a record number, were killed.

Probably never in history have there been days of shooting like those in October 1890 when the Prince of Wales visited his friend Baron Hirsch at St. Johann on the Austro-Hungarian border for a partridge shoot. The Baron, who employed several hundred beaters, had organized the shoot with remarkable skill. The results showed the superiority of his arrangements: in ten days an average of ten guns killed 20,000 partridges!

King Edward VII was also a great yachtsman, and he helped make the sport popular.

He patronized the track and won the Derby in 1896 with a horse named Persimmon.

The higher nobility of Great Britain followed his lead in these expensive and time-consuming occupations. It was a period when the territorial magnates were becoming ever richer while the country gentry, whose sport had been so much simpler, declined both in landholdings and in actual money. The British were celebrated for their interest in sports and their prowess at them. Clive Phillipps-Wolley, himself a noted shot, wrote complacently in 1894: "It is true that there is no big game left in Britain; but if the game is not British, its hunters are, and it is hardly too much to say that, out of every ten riflemen wandering about the world at present from Spitzbergen to Central Africa, nine are of the Anglo-Saxon breed."

British equipment for sportsmen, especially guns, was used everywhere. Sportsmen of many nations came to London to be outfitted for their expeditions. The high standards of British manufacturers have insured the durability of their products, and a large percentage of all the antiques of sport on the market today are British in origin.

Sport was just as actively pursued on the continent, but the style was different. In the old Austrian Empire, which ended in 1918, hunters managed things so that they were able to shoot nearly the whole year round. In August, they shot the chamois, which is a goatlike antelope found in the mountains. In the autumn and through the early winter they sought stag on the ground and partridge and pheasant in the air. The depths of the winter brought the season for bear and wild boar. Following that came the sport of stalking the capercailzies, wily birds that had to be shot while singing their mating song at dawn, which made it necessary for the sportsmen to get up between one and two in the morning and scramble uphill in the dark for hours just to get within range of them.

Establishments capable of preserving

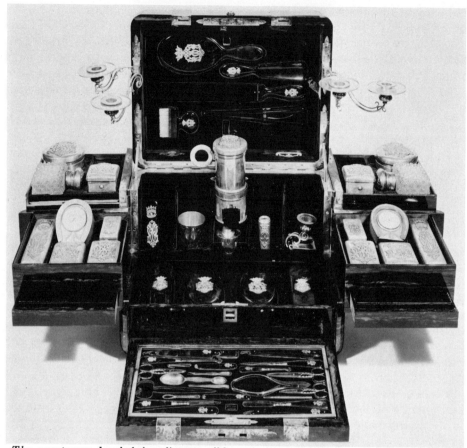

The sportsman headed for distant wild game grounds in the nineteenth century required not only a battery of guns but many articles for his personal convenience. It was an era of long trips and inexpensive shipping, and traveling cases of great ingenuity and completeness were available at the fine shops of London and Paris. This especially well equipped example of a gentleman's traveling case was made in 1880/81. It contains twelve silver boxes, two cut-glass bottles with silver covers, a shaving pot with lampstand and beaker for hot water, candlesticks, twenty-four tortoiseshell toilet and writing articles, and horseshoe-shaped barometer and alarm clock. Some of the fittings were made in Paris circa 1880. Others, matching, are English, made by W. Thornhill, 144 New Bond Street, and hallmarked London, 1881. The weighable silver amounts to 165 ounces. The chest itself is made from cala- mander wood with silver armorial markings; it was placed within a larger case of brassbound oak, placed in turn in a canvas trunk by Louis Vuitton for shipping. Collection of James F. Carr, New York

game on such a scale and of housing, feeding, and entertaining sportsmen for weeks on end naturally were maintained by only a few of the richest noblemen. The Prince of Liechtenstein employed more than a thousand gamekeepers. At the great Jubilee of the Emperor Franz Josef in Vienna in 1898 (his fiftieth year on the throne; as it turned out, he had eighteen years more!), one of the events was the *Waidmanns Huldigung*, Sportsmen's Homage. The large landowners brought their entire staffs of foresters and gamekeepers to be reviewed by the aged emperor, who himself was a great hunter. Each lord stood in front of his contingent. All five thousand were dressed in the Austrian gray and green shooting garb. After a review by Franz Josef, there was a great display of marksmanship—a *Schützenfest*.

The noblemen of Central Europe not only hunted and shot. Younger men were *Herrenreiter*, gentlemen riders. One of the most famous was Count Wilhelm Starhemberg, an Austrian of very high rank. He rode in 412 races, coming in first 87 times. In 1892, a great race for *Herrenreiter* was arranged from Vienna to Berlin and Berlin to Vienna. Entrants included 106 German riders and 93 Austrian. Count Starhemberg won by riding the 375 miles in 71 hours, 26 minutes.

Wilhelmine Germany, the empire of Kaiser Wilhelm II, was particularly notable for its interest in hunting. The great German families, enormously rich before the First World War, preserved game in quantity and killed it in such ceremonial state that their way of life seems almost mythical today. In fact, it passed away only fifty years ago, and there are people living now who participated in the great German hunts and shoots.

One of the most interesting changes in the development of sports has come about since the First World War. Although it is certainly possible to travel far for hunting and to spend a great deal of money on equipment, which has become more and more sophisticated, the immense slaughter of game is no longer carried on anywhere. The hunting man's idea of good sport has reverted to the comparatively small-scale outing described by Surtees a century and a half ago. Even if enormous kills were still possible under today's licensing laws, it is doubtful that many sportsmen would care to attend battues and engage in "drawing-room shooting." The antique equipment of Victorian and Edwardian days is popular with collectors, but there are few who envy the actual routine of those days.

In the United States in the nineteenth century, the sports remained simpler than in Europe. There was no ceremonial of hunting, much less battues. Americans, however, ardently took up the new or revived sports of the mid-century: archery, croquet, marksmanship, bicycling, lawn tennis. It was also the era when baseball and football, which were to become the great American spectator sports of the twentieth century, had their formal beginnings. Looking at nineteenth-century American sporting prints, which are easy to find even today, one is able to see which sports were most popular. As the prints were very widely distributed and as many (Currier and Ives, for example) were priced well in reach of most people, their subjects are good indications of those sports that were considered to have the most appeal. Horse racing was the most popular subject of American prints throughout the entire nineteenth century; shooting and, later, pugilism were not far behind. There are a few early American prints said to represent fox hunting on Long Island, but these are probably only copies of English prints touched up for the American market. Other sports depicted in prints were curling, bowling, swimming, skating, yachting, and, later, baseball and football.

The shooting and fishing prints give clear indication that those sports had just barely ceased to be necessity and become sport. None of the elaborate equipment used in Europe at that time is shown, and the sportsmen's costumes indicate how long a

Man o' War was one of the greatest racehorses of all time and a particular favorite of the public—they called him "Big Red." His lifespan was 1917–47, his racing seasons 1919/20. He ran in twenty-one races, of which he won twenty. Here he is winning the Stuyvesant Handicap at Jamaica on 22 June 1920, C. Kummer up. C. C. Cook, who specialized in recording racing with his camera, made this photograph. Keeneland Library, Lexington, Kentucky

The oldest trophy given for an American sporting event is the silver porringer awarded in 1668 for the horse race "runn at hanpsted plaines," (today Hempstead) Long Island. The maker was Peter van Inburgh. The original porringer is in the Yale University Art Gallery, but replicas have been made. Shown is one presented to the National Museum of Racing by the New York Racing Association to commemorate the 300th anniversary of racing in the United States. National Museum of Racing, Inc., Saratoga Springs, New York

period would elapse before Americans dressed in specific garb to pursue these sports: they engaged in hunting, shooting, and fishing for the sake of the game taken or the recreation. It was not yet the era of "sports clothes." The hunter of nineteenth-century America required only his gun and the fisherman only his rod and possibly high boots. It is revealing that most of the great hunting parties that visited the game regions of America during the nineteenth century were organized by wealthy foreigners—for example, the Grand Duke Alexis of Russia in the 1870s (Buffalo Bill Cody was his guide).

There was a much smaller class of leisured sportsmen; American men still devoted much time to making money, regardless of how lavishly they also spent it. Sports, on the whole, were more democratic than in Europe. America was to be the first country where sporting events drew enormous crowds.

The first sport to be watched by armies of spectators was horse racing. The sport has a very long history in the United States, as noted earlier; it was the first sport to be "organized." The premier course was on Long Island, laid out in the 1660s by order of the first English governor of the colony of New York (but at one time races were also run on the Bowery, much to the annoyance of its residents). Both the important early American sporting periodicals —the *American Turf Register and Sporting Magazine* (published 1829–44) and *The Spirit of the Times* (1831–61)—were devoted mainly to the annals of horse racing. Americans loved, and still love, a fast horse. The English sportsman might prefer a hunter that could jump a fence or a ditch, but the Americans liked a horse that could hold its own on a course.

The first trotting match in America appears to have been run in 1818, a race against time for $1,000 to a horse that could trot a mile in three minutes. The New York Trotting Club was formed in 1825 to improve the speed of the horses; it first offered purses in the spring of 1826. Their first course, like that for the flats, was on Long Island. Races were run under saddle as well as in harness for many years. The use of the low-wheeled sulky is comparatively modern —the sulky is not shown in the old prints, but it appears in chromolithographs of the 1890s.

Another sport with a long history in the United States, which, like horse racing, requires its devotees to be rich, is yachting. Even at the turn of the nineteenth century there were yachtsmen in this country, the most famous being Captain George Crowninshield, Jr., whose twenty-two-ton sloop *Jefferson* was built in 1801. For more than a century and a half American yachtsmen have set the standard for the world, as evidenced by this country's continued possession of yachting's premier trophy, the America's Cup. The heyday of the sport was the late nineteenth century.

Frank Gray Griswold, who engaged in and wrote about nearly every American sport of his time, reminisced in his memoirs that 1865 to 1873 were the best years for all sports in the United States. "During those years the sportsman was favored by nature, and was not hampered by foolish laws. Game was plentiful and striped-bass fishing at its best . . . Pigeon shooting was not taboo, and there was great competition between the different strains of gamecocks, while boxing was the manly art of self-defense."

In 1901, William Patten edited a huge volume entitled *The Book of Sport* to which the leading American sportsmen and sportswomen contributed articles on the sports then in vogue. Spectator sports such as the ball games were ignored. The participatory sports described and illustrated were the following: golf; court tennis and related games such as racquets and squash; polo; fox hunting and drag hunting (following a laid-down scent with hounds); coaching; automobiling (still a sport then, not a neces-

Tiffany & Co. made this silver punch bowl trophy as "The Goelet Prize for Sloops 1899." Ogden Goelet, who donated the trophy, was one of the best-known American yachtsmen of the late nineteenth century. Gift of Mrs. C. Oliver Iselin, Museum of the City of New York

sity); lawn tennis; and yachting. Women are shown in the book very actively engaged in not only golf but also lawn tennis, fox hunting, and automobiling.

An interesting contrast is the 1974 list of sports considered the "most popular in the United States in terms of fan interest." Ranked from the top, they were:

football
baseball
basketball
tennis
auto racing
horse racing
boxing
track and field
hockey
boating

The modern Olympic games were revived at Athens in 1896. They have been held con-

Early vehicles used in the sport of motoring are beginning to attract collectors' interest at a high level of prices. Shown is a 1913 Mercer Raceabout. Sotheby Parke Bernet New York.

Fine equipment for the sportsman has long been purveyed by America's most famous sporting goods establishment, Abercrombie & Fitch. It was already at its present location (Madison Avenue and 45th Street) in New York when Byron photographed its well-supplied gun department. Note the fine trophy heads then decorating the store. The Byron Collection, Museum of the City of New York

tinuously since that time, always on a larger and larger scale and with a constantly increasing number of sports represented. The effect of this revival was to bring new attention to sports everywhere. The era of spectator sports had begun—with its enormous crowds of fans, publicity, and innumerable souvenirs. At the same time, many of the old sports like horse racing continued popular and comparatively new sports like lawn tennis were much more widely played.

Even such a brief survey as this of the history of sports in Europe and America makes it clear that the number of sports engaged in and the number of participants have sharply increased since the late eighteenth century. The increase became particularly noticeable in the latter half of the nineteenth century. In the twentieth century the emphasis of the sports-minded has

The National Baseball Hall of Fame and Museum at Cooperstown, New York, contains innumerable relics of the American national game. The trophy shown on the pedestal at left is the Temple Cup.
National Baseball Hall of Fame and Museum, Inc.

come to rest on the spectator sports, especially the team sports.

Since the late nineteenth century was the great age of widespread participation in sports, notably in those that require considerable equipment, such as the horse sports, shooting, and fishing, the average sports antique found today is likely to have been made in that era. It was a time in England and America when objects made for sportsmen, whether handcrafted or machine-made, were skillfully and conscientiously made, and made to last. There are sound reasons for the existence today of so many fine guns, harnesses, and fishing rods.

The importance of Anglo-American leadership in the history of most sports popular today is also apparent from the survey, and it is equally apparent in the sports antiques that survive. In the nineteenth and twentieth centuries British and American manufacturers have supplied most of the world with its sports equipment. To the collector of sports antiques in either the United States or Great Britain, the names of makers mentioned in this book will often be immediately recognizable, since a surprisingly large number are still actively engaged in making fine sports equipment that will be tomorrow's collectibles.

The stamp designs were also cast as medallions in silver, bronze, and gold. Pictured is a bronze set in its presentation case. The issue was produced by the Jacques Cartier Mint, Toronto. Canada Post Office

The modern Olympic Games have called forth many issues of commemorative items. When Montreal was selected as the site of the 1976 summer games, the Canadian government began to issue special coins and stamps, to be sold to collectors to raise funds for staging the Olympics. The special stamps shown here, issued in 1973, incorporate in their design the traditional symbol of the Games, five different-colored circles on a field of white, representing the five continents. Canada Post Office

2

ANTIQUES OF THE HORSE SPORTS

Horsemen have long delighted in fine accouterments for their animals. The magnificent armor and other trappings in which medieval knights decked their horses for tournaments often served as much for decoration as for protection. Horse furnishings of the late Middle Ages and Renaissance are considered part of the collecting field of arms and armor. The only horse equipment of those periods the collector will be likely to see is that displayed in museums. Like most other categories of armor, the fine linked metal or padded armor and leather and metal harness worn by the steeds in both war and tournaments have become so extremely rare that they are hardly collectible today. The sales of armor that are held, mostly in London and continental cities, consist mainly of museum duplicates and surplus; the buyers, for the most part, are other arms and armor museums. The armor on the market now usually consists of the merest bits and pieces. Full suits for man or horse have disappeared into institutions.

In the area of textile collecting there are a number of items that can be considered as horse antiques. From the most ancient times many peoples of the Near East and Central Asia have woven fine textiles for use as saddlecloths, saddlebags, and cinches. The saddlecloths, also called saddle rugs, are especially noted for their colors and designs. All these textiles are actively collected, but as examples of weaving art; there are few collectors who would regard this as an area of sports collecting.

Modern horse sports—that is, those that have been popular since the eighteenth century—require a good deal of equipment for the horse and its rider. Much of this is of fairly recent origin, mainly nineteenth century, because in that century all the horse sports greatly increased in popularity. A pattern familiar in many areas of collecting is repeated: as the horse was slowly making its departure as the indispensable means for transport, there was a final burst of horse activity and a consequent accumulation of collectibles. Many of the most famous organized horse events in the United States, for example, had their beginning in the last third of the nineteenth century. The Kentucky Derby was first run in 1874. The National Horse Show at Madison Square Garden started in 1885; well into the present century it was considered the opening of the New York social season for the "sporting set." The American Jockey Club was established in 1866; the famous racing stables like the Lorillard, Whitney, Widener, and others were organized soon after by various rich families. The Meadowbrook Hunt Club on Long Island and other organized hunts date to the 1880s. Many of these activities are thriving today.

The most collectible antique of the horse is the saddle. It developed out of a cloth laid over the horse's back for the rider's comfort and safety. Only gradually did it come to be made of leather in Europe; saddles that are woven or made of wood are still in use in many parts of the world. Neither the ancient Greeks nor the Romans used saddles until, perhaps, very near the end of the Roman imperial period. A saddle is, of course, not necessary for riding, as countless bareback riders through the ages have proved. Entire cultures producing great horsemen, such as the American Plains Indians, have done so without benefit of the saddle; there remain places today where riders do not use saddles.

In Europe the saddle came into use very early in the Middle Ages. The balance and steadiness that the saddle provides made possible the furious horseback activities of the medieval knights—war, tournaments, and hunting. The very high pommel and cantle (front and back of seat) on medieval saddles were originally introduced to hold the rider on during jousting. They were very slow to pass out of saddlery design. Stirrups were also regularly used in medieval times. Actual examples of saddles are known to exist in England from at least Elizabethan times (the sixteenth century). These are made of leather ornamented with appliqués of leather and brass nails. None of these is now likely to be seen outside a museum.

There are various categories of saddles based on their construction, and many varieties within each. Nearly every great horse-based culture has developed its own special saddle. In Anglo-American civilization the two principal types of saddles have long been the "English" and the "Western." The English saddle has no horn, the Western does; the English is padded but the Western is hard; the stirrup is hung farther forward on the English style than on the Western. The racing saddle used today is an English type; a cowboy's saddle is the Western—cowboys need the high horn for using their lassos. There is an American saddle without a horn called the "McClellan type," developed during the Civil War by the Union general George B. McClellan. It is especially attractive to collectors because of its Civil War associations and because it was long used by the United States Cavalry; it therefore figures in the history of the Western frontier and Indian fighting. The "sidesaddle," in which the rider sits with both legs on the same side (usually the horse's left), was used in England as early as the twelfth century. It has always been

Will Rogers, a famous rider and an expert with the lariat, formed a huge collection of antiques relating to the horse sports; it is now at the Will Rogers Memorial Commission at his birthplace in Oklahoma. The small and miniature saddles in his collection, made in various styles, were from many parts of the world. Will Rogers Memorial Commission, Claremore, Oklahoma

the woman's saddle in European civilization, although in some Near Eastern countries camels are ridden sidesaddle by men.

Fine saddlery has been a product of the United States Southwest, Mexico, and southern South America since the early days of the Spanish colonial settlements. Spanish settlers brought with them a very ancient tradition of horsemanship that showed Arabian influence from the long Moorish domination of the Iberian peninsula. In the New World cattle were raised on such a large scale that there was a continuous supply of hides to be worked into fine saddles and harness. In addition, in Mexico and some parts of South America, there was a fabulous amount of silver available for ornamenting the leatherwork and for making stirrups and spurs. No saddles

used by the early Spanish settlers of the American Southwest are known to exist, but there are many nineteenth- and twentieth-century saddles made in the traditional manner that are collectors' items today.

The most elaborate Mexican saddles belong to the so-called *charro* outfits. *Charro* is a Spanish word meaning "rustic" or "boorish," but it has taken on special significance in connection with the Mexican and southwestern men who get themselves and their horses up in an especially elaborate outfit, a costume really, using much fine leather with silver decoration. The Mexican *charro* saddle has a low, raking cantle and pommel and a flat, thick horn. Those made in Mexico and Spanish California, hand-tooled with leather roses on the skirts and the straps of the saddle and adorned with all sorts of silver trimmings, are much sought today and command substantial prices, although the market is for the most part regional.

Charro saddles are often made with matching spurs and a machete, the large, heavy knife used in clearing paths. Also of fine workmanship are the accompanying bridles (made of rawhide) and the metal chain attaching the reins to the bit. The leather leggings worn by horsemen are stamped with elaborate patterns and even embroidered with gold or silver thread and sometimes lined with colored velvet. The entire costume, worn by riders in parades and horse shows today, is a glittering sight indeed.

In Argentina the *gaucho* saddle is a famous product of the cattle-raising industry of the country. A gaucho saddle looks like a pack on the horse's back. It consists of reeds, felt, and wool with leather mounts and cinches. Formless at first, it takes on the shape of the cowboy's body. Attached to it are *bolos*, which are weights or balls on the ends of leather strips. These are thrown at running cattle and other animals, entangling their feet and thus bringing them down. The blankets that accompany these saddles are often extremely elaborate. In Argentina and other parts of South America, fine silver stirrups have been made since colonial times. On gaucho saddles they are often very small, for "toe-riding"—that is, for resting the rider's feet in lightly rather than thrusting them in deeply. Such stirrups are attached to the saddle by silver rods rather than stirrup leathers.

Many antique American saddles are in existence. A glance at almost any old catalogue will accurately demonstrate the importance of the horse in American life until about fifty years ago. In 1902, the huge Sears, Roebuck catalogue gave over 10 percent of its entire space to horse-related items. It is interesting to note that saddles were priced between $4.85 and $31.85; the higher price was for a luxury item. Saddles

In this room the various trappings of the horse are displayed on the walls—bridles, stirrups, hobbles, and lariats. A wall not shown holds Rogers's polo mallet and outfit. Will Rogers Memorial Commission, Claremore, Oklahoma

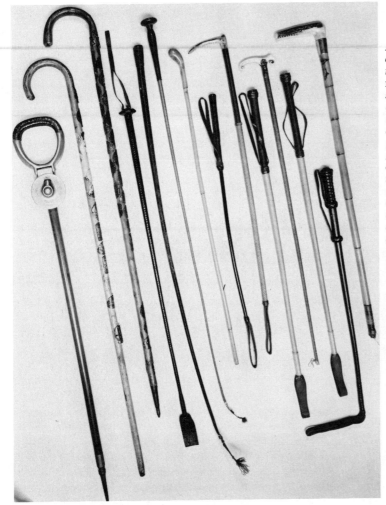

A shooting stick, walking sticks, and a variety of crops and whips for the rider are shown here. From left to right: an English-made shooting stick, 33 inches long, of mahogany-colored wood with aluminum fittings and seat, including a detachable guard for preventing the stick from penetrating too far into the ground; two Alpine walking sticks, each with metal plaques engraved with names and views of various towns visited on a walking tour in Central Europe in the nineteenth century (when a tourist reached a new town he bought a plaque and had it mounted on his walking stick as a memento of his visit); riding crop with braided leather body; dressage whip of braided flax with etched sterling silver head with raised initials; another dressage whip with sterling silver head; bamboo riding crop; an unusual riding crop with a silver-headed alligator-leather handle and tortoiseshell body; riding crop with antler-head handle; English riding crop with cap handle; braided thread riding whip with sterling silver and ivory handle; two leather riding crops; stag head riding crop with bamboo body, 27½ inches in length. Collection of James F. Carr, New York

of American origin, unless McClellan, southwestern, or of special historical interest, such as having been the property of a noted person, have been little collected. Since large numbers of them are known to exist, they offer a field for the modest or beginning collector.

Whips and riding crops, which are usually made of leather, are frequently collected. They are small and can make an attractive wall display. The handles or butts are often made of silver, initialed or with heraldic devices. Those used by the British military forces are particularly handsome. Among

the other substances that have been used for the handle is scrimshaw; such crops date from the first half of the nineteenth century. Today crops often have a fiber glass center covered with calfskin or pigskin. The handle may be in the "staghorn" form, resembling an antler. The thongs are generally made of leather with a silk lash at the end. The loop at the top of a riding crop for the attaching of the thong is called a "keeper." English riding whips often have a right-angled crook on the handle, usually with corrugations on each side, for assistance in opening and shutting gates. (Traditionally,

Horse racing was depicted by many of the very greatest artists of the nineteenth century. Edgar Degas was almost as fascinated by racing scenes as he was by ballet rehearsals. Here is one of his very small racing paintings (oil on canvas, 8 x 10 inches) entitled merely Jockeys.

many English gates have been made so that they can be opened and closed by a person on horseback.) The short whips used by jockeys are known as "bats."

Although complete bridles are not usually very attractive to collectors, the rosettes made to hang on and ornament bridles are. Most rosettes date from the second half of the nineteenth century. They were made of glass, horn, brass, copper, gilded lead, and other metals. The glass rosettes were hollow and had animal or flower designs under the glass. Metal rosettes were decorated with an endless variety of subjects, including horses, dogs, tigers, eagles, initials, heraldic crests and other devices, club ornaments and emblems, and bull's-eyes. Those with royal or regimental arms are particularly sought, but the glass-covered rosettes are perhaps the most decorative.

Horse racing is a sport with an unusually fine iconograpy. The literature of racing is

also large: most of the classic books on horses have emphasized the Thoroughbred racing horses. A notable example is the eccentric but indispensable work by Lady Wentworth called *The Authentic Arabian Horse and His Descendants* (London, 1945). Racing offers less for the antique collector, excepting trophies, than other horse sports. The hunt, because it requires more equipment for the rider, is a larger field in antique collecting.

Racing silks (i.e., the colored cap and blouse of jockeys or harness-race drivers) are to be seen on display in museums devoted to racing and trotting. They are an unusual antique in that it is possible precisely to date the introduction of individual racing silks to distinguish the various horses during meets. Their first use was during the October 1762 races at Newmarket in England. On that occasion seventeen gentlemen who had horses running came together to register individual colors "for greater con-

C. C. Cook's photographic archives at the Keeneland Library contain many remarkable shots of unusual happenings on the track. Here is a jockey named Stone taking a tumble off Sandalwood at the Gravesend, Long Island, track on 10 June 1907. Keeneland Library, Lexington, Kentucky

Many sports anniversaries and personalities have been commemorated philatelically. This First Day of Issue Cover honoring (here "honouring") the 100th Anniversary of the running of the Kentucky Derby was issued on 4 May 1974. The "cachet" (decoration) at left is by the sporting artist Henry Koehler.

venience in distinguishing horses in the running and to prevent disputes." The seventeen represented quite a cross section of the
peerage, since six were dukes, one a marquis,
five were earls, and all but two of the re-
mainder were titled, a good indication of
the social prestige of sport in that era. In
the two succeeding centuries there have
been only slight changes made in the colors
chosen for the various stables. Some of them
remain on the turf today—for example, the
Grosvenor (dukes of Westminster) "yellow,
and black cap" and Lord Derby's "black,
white cap."

Fox hunting became a great English sport
during the eighteenth century. All horse
sports became more widespread and popular
in England at that period, in large part because the horses were better. The Arabian
horse had been introduced into the country
in late Stuart times. It was much faster
than the old breeds; the Arabian blood
developed the Thoroughbred running on the
world's tracks today. Superior horses then
became available in England for training as
hunters. Just as important was the decline
of the old sport of staghunting. That sport
gradually faded as the population increased
all over the British Isles. More land was
fenced and placed under cultivation to produce food for these new people. The old
England had been quite heavily wooded and
ideal for hunting deer with hounds. Now the
fox hunt began to take its place. Actually,
the old chronicles show that before about
1750 when hunters rode out with hounds
they usually pursued whatever came to
hand—stag, hares, or foxes. There was great
state for the hunt itself, but little snobbery
about the quarry.

Today, stags are generally stalked, but in
Ireland one or two clubs still hunt the stag
with hounds. The stags are, however,
brought to the field "boxed," let loose, pursued, and captured rather than killed so
they can be hunted another day.

Between about 1750 and the turn of the

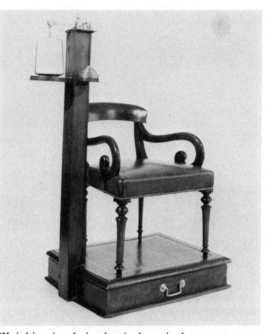

*Weighing-in chairs for jockeys in horse races are
a rare form of furniture dating to the eighteenth
century. This mahogany example with leather
seat is from early nineteenth-century England. The
weighing mechanism is concealed under the plat-
form, which has a false drawer front. The original
weights are in "stones" rather than pounds. Otto
Zenke, Inc.*

nineteenth century all the most important
packs of hounds in England changed over
from staghounds to harriers or fox hounds.
Family packs of hounds were established at
that time, the blood of which continues in
hounds used today. The Brocklesby Hunt's
hound lists go back to 1746; they are probably the oldest in existence.

As for the age of the hunts themselves,
the celebrated Quorn Hunt claims to be the
oldest. This claim rests in large part on an
interesting relic, a hunting horn on which
is engraved:

Thos. Boothby, Esq., Tooley Park, Leicester.
With this horn he hunted the first pack of
fox-hounds then in England 55 years. Born
1677 died 1752

Fox hunting has an American history

The Quorn Hunt claims to be the oldest established fox-hunting pack in England, dating back to the first half of the eighteenth century. This engraving showing Sir Richard Sutton and the Quorn Hounds in the nineteenth century was made after a painting by Sir Francis Grant, who was President of the Royal Academy in 1866 and noted for his portrayals of hunting scenes. Phillips Auctioneers, London

quite as long but not so organized or well documented as England's. George Washington loved fox hunting, and it was widely engaged in during the late colonial and early federal eras. A hunt was advertised in Brooklyn in November 1791 that offered a reward: "A guinea or more will be given for a good strong Bag Fox," meaning a fox to be let loose for the chase. Another party had a "fine chace round Fort Washington," near where the Cloisters Museum in New York now stands.

The direct ancestors of present-day fox hunting in the United States are hunts like the Radnor (1884) near Philadelphia and the Genesee Valley (1876) in western New York. Great difficulties had to be overcome to establish American fox hunting: American foxes are larger and wilder than those in Britain and require different hounds; the

best hunt country, such as upstate New York, is subject to heavy snow in the months when the foxes are reputed to run best (January and February); and in many parts of the country the fences are wire, making jumping impossible. Nevertheless, hunting was successfully established and has been maintained here as it is in England and Ireland to the present day.

As noted earlier, few sports required a special costume before the nineteenth century. Almost the only exception to this was at the royal courts, where a livery was worn, indeed required, and a special hunt costume gradually developed. In his book on hunting, Gaston Phoebus refers to uniforms of green worn for staghunting and of gray for boar hunting. At some royal establishments courtiers were ordered to don coats of a particular design and color to accompany the monarch on the chase. Henry IV of France went hunting in a red cloak, perhaps the earliest red garb associated with the hunt.

Wearing special clothing of different colors to engage in a sport gradually became the custom, seeping down from the royal establishments. Fox hunting outfits have such a history. Although the "pink" (actually, scarlet) coat is synonymous now with riding to hounds, it was not always considered indispensable, and indeed today there are long-established hunts that wear other colors. The tradition developed very slowly although the distinction was preserved—as it is today—between "livery" worn by the hunt servants and "uniforms" worn by members of the hunt. The famous Lady Salisbury, who bred dwarf foxhounds at her historic house Hatfield, in Hertfordshire, and was a Master of the Fox Hounds in the late eighteenth century, used to dress her field in sky-blue uniforms with black collars, lapels, and jockey caps. George Washington hunted in a blue coat, scarlet waistcoat, buckskin breeches, top boots, and velvet cap, and used a whip with a long thong.

One necessity of the hunter's costume avidly collected today is the sporting buttons worn on his coat. In the nineteenth century, when they had their greatest popularity, they were generally made of gold, silver, or silver plate, although examples are known in many other substances. The earliest known hunt buttons are a set of twenty-four in various sizes, hallmarked 1738. Animal heads, hunting horns, spurs, and other equipment are depicted on the buttons. Some coursing buttons have the name of a specific hound engraved and even its portrait. Buttons were also made for rac-

ing fanciers with the names of notable horses. In fact, sports from cockfighting to pigsticking were shown on the buttons, and they were worn by followers of all these sports. One firm, Allen & Moore, in England is known to have made more than three thousand different dies for buttons in the three years from 1848 to 1851. Buttons showing various sports, including hunt club buttons, are made to order today, and many are collectors' items now.

Another antique of the hunt is the well-known and very keenly collected form of silver known as the stirrup cup. It derives its name from the old custom of the farewell drink given to a departing dinner guest leaving on horseback. It was the ancient equivalent of "one for the road," and was especially the custom during the hard-drinking eighteenth and early nineteenth centuries. The outdoor men of the time were not dainty about their consumption of hard liquor. Nimrod recalled that it was not unusual in his youth to see a guest so drunk that he had to be lifted onto his horse "yet not suffered to depart without this finish to the feast which he took after he was seated in his saddle." Needless, serious, and even fatal accidents were fairly common occurrences on homeward trips.

Later the term "stirrup cup" came to be applied to a small variety of silver tumbler about three inches high, which held a single drink for consumption by a hunter while mounted. Hunters might pause at a roadside inn in their pursuit of the fox and have their stirrup cups to refresh them. The most familiar form of the cups is the fox-mask shape, which began to be made in the second half of the eighteenth century. It is extremely realistic in depicting the fox's mask, which is usually shown with a snarling expression. Around the head may be a collar engraved with a fox-hunting cry or the slogan of a hunt. Most silver fox-mask stirrup cups were made before 1830. Silver stirrup cups were also made in hound-mask form at about the same period and in the

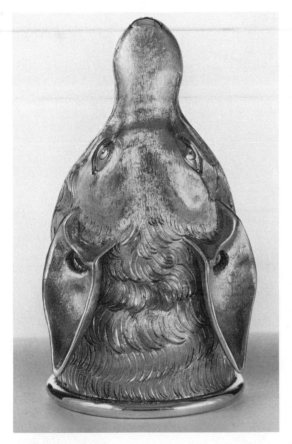

Silver stirrup cup made in the form of a fox mask, London, 1807/8, by W. Burwash and R. Sibley. It is 5¾ inches long—an exceedingly fine example. Victoria and Albert Museum. Crown Copyright

form of racehorse heads in the early Victorian period.

Stirrup cups in fox- or hound-mask form have also been made in earthenware (especially by Whieldon and Ralph Wood) and in porcelain at Chelsea, Derby, Coalport, and other factories in England. These are executed with varying amounts of skill and taste. The most attractively done—and the most expensive—are those made by Chelsea.

One of the most interesting antiques of the chase is the hunting horn. This delightful instrument grew out of the shell or animal horn or tusk through which, in early times, men blew a loud blast to attract hunters (or warriors) of a party who had got beyond the reach of the human voice.

The fox-hunters' horn used in the field for centuries is probably the closest wind instrument to the remote ancestor of shell or horn. Only one note can be blown on it,

and so, to achieve different calls, long and short blasts on the horn are necessary. Closely related to the bugle, the post horn, and to coach horns of various types, this instrument is bent into circular shape so that it can be looped over the arm for convenience while riding or holding hounds on leash. In English it is called the hunting horn; in German, the *Waldhorn*, and in French, the *cor de chasse*. Orchestrally, the hunting horn is the ancestor of the French horn.

The horn is used to notify the field what game is started, to give warning, to encourage the hounds, and to tell widely dispersed hunters what the circumstances of the hunt are. There are about thirty-one recognized "hunting calls," most of them of French origin. King Louis XIII of France invented a special call to be used only for the fox, and many of those used today were invented by King Louis XV and his master of the hunt about a century later. The military reveille is the most familiar of these calls. There are horn "fanfares" to identify each animal such as the wolf, wild boar, fox, weasel, hare, and several for the stag, varying according to his age and antlers. Louis XV invented the "royal fanfare" for a stag of ten points. The third class of hunting airs are those performed after a successful hunt while the bag is being displayed.

In the nineteenth century the "English hunt horn" used in fox hunting came into general use in England and America. It is still made today. About ten inches long and straight, like a coach horn, it is generally made of copper, although other metals have been used, including silver. Horns are kept

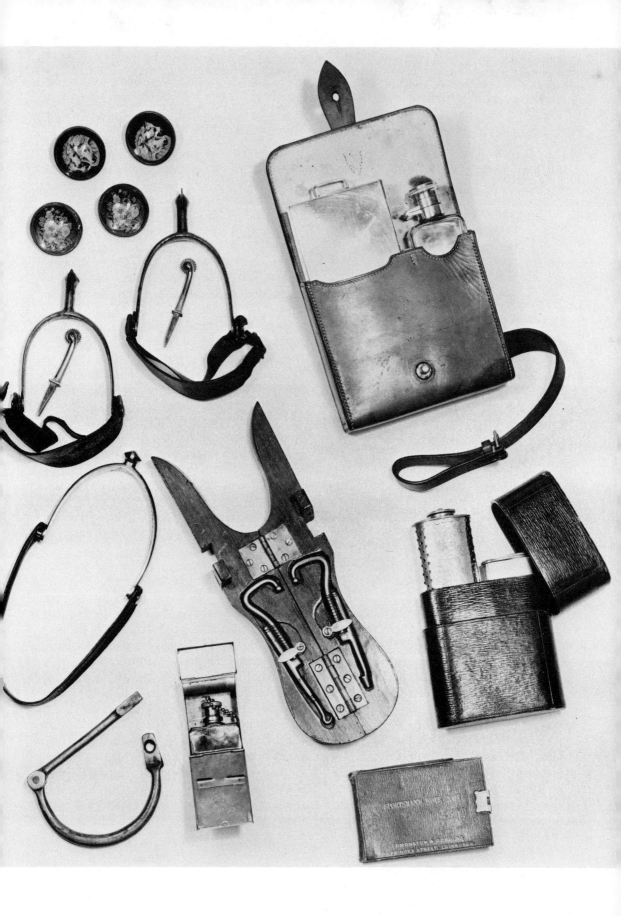

Opposite page

Antique equipment for the horse sports includes (beginning top left): *four glass bridle rosettes with floral designs; two pair of spurs, those with leather thongs for fitting around the boots of the rider, the others for fitting into the boots; a leather hunt canteen (5 x 5¾ inches) containing a sandwich box and glass flask, made in England; a stainless steel spur made by Swaine & Adeney; a set of boot hooks in a wooden case, which is a bootjack when open (as shown) 11¼ inches long, formerly the property of the Duc de Richelieu; a handwarmer in leather case (5½ x 4 inches) made by Instra, 47 Cannon Street, London, with refill case for powdered charcoal and safety pin attachment for hanging warmer within garments; a brass bit used as a lead; another type of handwarmer, this one using lighter fluid, made by M. D. Pioneer, New York; the Sportsman's Note Book, at bottom, made by the firm of Edmonston & Douglas of Princes Street, Edinburgh, also belonging to the Duc de Richelieu, which contains his shooting record for Fall 1890, listing the game (mostly rabbit) shot at his country home.* Collection of James F. Carr, New York

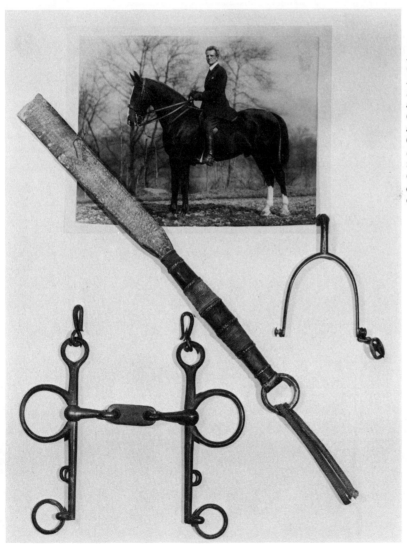

The distinguished German-American photographer Arnold Genthe was an ardent horseman. Here he is mounted on Chesty, his favorite horse, which is described in As I Remember, Genthe's autobiography. The self-photograph was taken in Central Park, New York. The bit, spur (the "Prince of Wales" type), and crop are those in Genthe's photograph, which dates from the 1920s. Collection of James F. Carr, New York

in elegant leather cases. Most of the collectible hunting horns found today are these "English hunt horns."

Among the many antique "appointments" for the fox hunter are hunt canteens made of leather, containing a metal sandwich box and a glass or metal flask; leather saddle pouches for holding glasses and other small objects; many varieties of flasks with leather cases, with straps for attaching to the saddle; and even wire cutters, used to open wire fences, the bane of the hunter. These were about six inches long and came encased in leather pouches. All this equipment was produced in the nineteenth century, most of it in high-quality materials. Much of it has been preserved.

Here is a sampling of the many horse antiques that are collectible, with some price ranges of the early 1970s:

- Bridle rosettes
brass:	$5–$10
copper:	$10–$20
glass:	$10

- Harness, many accessories, usually of brass or brass-tipped leather, such as collars, bits, hames (fasteners for traces), curbs, hitching weights, etc.: $10–$25

- Saddles unless silver-decorated or otherwise unusual $100

- Sporting buttons
brass:	$10
copper:	$15
silver:	$25+

- Spurs
iron:	$10–$200
silver:	$250+

- Stirrups
brass:	$50–$75
silver-ornamented:	$250+

- Stirrup cups
silver, Georgian:	$2,000+
silver, Regency:	$1,000+
earthenware, e.g., Ralph Wood:	$300+

- Hunt horns, copper: $10–$25
  Silver horns, which are usually engraved with name of the hunt or a hunter and are often presentation pieces to a Master of Fox Hounds, naturally sell for much more. Any horn is more desirable if it is preserved in its original leather case.

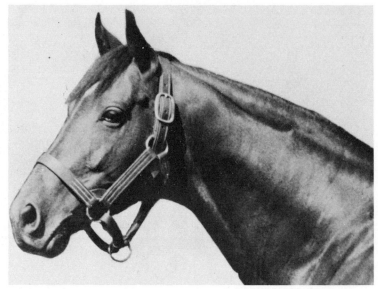

Many owners of fine horses have used a subject chosen from their own stables to picture on their Christmas cards. Shown on this card is Princequillo, bred in Ireland, who was raced in the United States in the colors of the Boone Hall Stable. In 1957 and 1958 he was the leading sire. Photograph loaned by James F. Carr, New York

Despite the difficulties of a terrain and climate quite different, for the most part, from the great fox-hunting areas of England and Ireland, hunting is well established in the United States. There is a National Steeplechase and Hunt Association (founded in 1895) and, as of 1975, about 140 recognized hunts. Sixteen are in the tri-state area around New York City, but the growth in recent years has been in the Southern states. Here is an American hunt with its huntsman, field, and dogs, returning from a run. Photograph loaned by James F. Carr, New York

3

ANGLING AND SHOOTING ANTIQUES

FISHING TACKLE

Few sports can be so simply practiced as fishing, yet few can
utilize such a quantity of equipment. Angling can require only the simplest of rods,
lines, and hooks, and the humble worm as
bait, but at the same time a range of angling
accouterments is available, probably broader
than that of any other widely practiced
individual sport. These have become so
sophisticated and specialized that in fishing
tournaments today a boat may have an
oxygen monitor for locating places where
there are so many parts of oxygen per million parts of water, along with a water ther-
mometer, contour maps of bodies of water,
and an electronic depth finder, all of course
to assist the fisherman in finding the fish.

There are now professional anglers who fish
in tournaments for a living and employ these
extraordinary devices, although some tournament fishermen still rely on intuition and
experience.

Fishing for food and even for sport is old
beyond knowledge, but most of the "antique" equipment is relatively quite modern
—overwhelmingly nineteenth century in
origin. Few pieces, in fact, date to before
1850. In ethnological museums, along with
arrowheads and other implements of ancient
man, the visitor will see very ancient fishhooks made of iron, bronze, or ivory. Only
rarely can such items be exactly identified
as to origin; they are primarily of anthro-
pological interest.

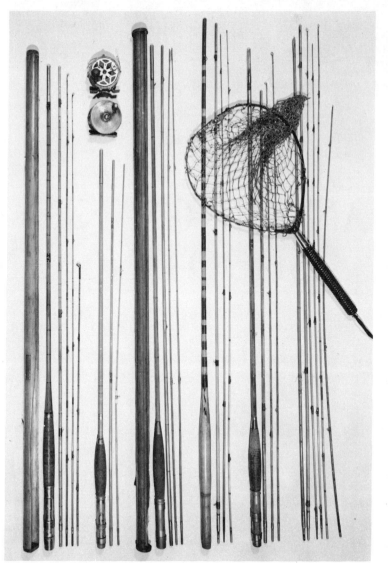

A group of antique fishing rods, some with their carrying cases, and detachable parts; reels, closed and ventilated; and a net ring and handle, the ring made by Hawco, the detachable handle by Winchester. The rod at farthest left was made in the late nineteenth century for Mrs. Daniel H. Kane by B. F. Nichols, H. C. Litchfield & Co. of Boston and has a silver butt with her initials engraved on it. The extensions of the rod are also initialed. Among the other rods are several made for Prince Alexander Hohenlohe of the German family well-known for its sportsmen. Several of the rods are split bamboo. Collection of James F. Carr, New York

Old angling equipment of American origin exists. The fishing tackle of George Washington, who was a devoted fisherman, is preserved at Mount Vernon. Advertisements in old American newspapers show that there was manufacturing and commerce in supplies for fishermen at least in the pre-Revolutionary era. Watson and Murray in New York City advertised in 1765 that they had fishhooks made by William Sheward in Pennsylvania. They boasted that Sheward's "are equal if not superior in Quality to any imported from Europe; and always free from Rust, which by the frequent Damps in Vessels, European made are always liable to." And in the first year of the nineteenth century James Amory of No. 71 Water Street, New York, a whipmaker, advertised that he sold guns and "some salmon and trout Rods, of an approved plan, with rules, lines, flies etc." Such items, identifiable as to period and maker, are virtually never available to the collector today.

RODS. Until after mid-nineteenth century, fishing rods were made from wood; very occasionally whalebone or native cane was employed. Very few makers of wooden rods can be named. The oldest rod at the American Museum of Fly Fishing in Manchester, Vermont, is inscribed and dated 1832, but the maker is unknown. Kenneth M. Cameron, an expert on the history of American fly rods, says that among the outstanding wooden-rod makers working in the third quarter of the nineteenth century were "Robert Welch, the Pritchard Brothers, and most important of all, William Mitchell (died circa 1887), all of New York City." Many tackle houses sold anonymously made rods. Most rods were made of native woods —hickory, ash, maple; often more than one wood was used.

Split-bamboo rods were introduced in the late 1860s. They were expensive then, as they are now. The bamboo itself was imported, and a number of operations were required to make the rod. These rods are excellent antiques for collectors, as they are often identifiable, carrying patent dates and the name of the maker. The premier American rodmaker and the one whose product is most wanted by collectors was H. L. Leonard, first of Bangor, Maine, and then Cen-

tral Valley, New York, working from 1870 on.

The study of nineteenth-century rodmakers is only now in progress and their names being discovered. The following list includes both individual makers and tackle houses whose names may be found, generally, on the butt of the rod. It includes those that will most likely be sought by collectors.

Abbey & Imbrie, New York
Anderson, Edinburgh
A. Carter & Co., London
Thomas H. Chubb, Post Mills, Vermont
Cross Rod Co., Lynn, Massachusetts
Farlow, London
H. L. Leonard, Bangor, Maine, and Central Valley, N.Y.
William Mitchell & Son, New York
B. F. Nichols, Boston
Charles F. Orvis Co., Manchester, Vermont
C. E. Wheeler, New York City

On the above list, the name of Orvis is particularly famous in the annals of fishing

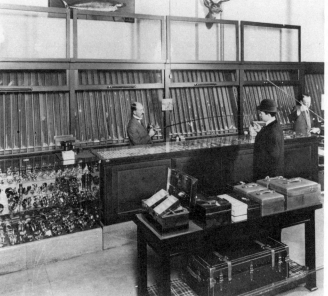

The fishing tackle department at Abercrombie & Fitch about 1912 as photographed by Byron. Note demonstrations by salesmen and fine tackle cases on display table. The Byron Collection, Museum of the City of New York

tackle. The firm bearing the name of the Orvis family of Manchester, Vermont, is still in business although under different ownership; it is now the leading direct-mail tackle business in the United States. Orvis is still making bamboo rods, using cane from the Wai Tsap district of Kwangsi Province in China.

Enough fine antique fishing rods can be found to make them a collectible field. There are some curiosities for the collector, too, such as "walking stick rods," which— according to nineteenth-century manufacturers—looked so much like a cane or walking stick that they had "not the least appearance of a Fishing-Rod." Along with the rods a good many rod cases have survived. These were made of wood, canvas, or leather, some in a telescope form.

REELS. A crude form of reel made of wood is said to date from the fifteenth century. In the old literature of angling the reel is often called a "wind," a "winch," or a "wheeler." On old rods the reel was placed a foot or more up the butt, and it was smaller than today because casts were relatively short and little line needed to be stored. The line was made of grass, horsehair, or silk. Reels fastened to rods with band and thumbscrew were in use until the late 1880s; about that time the reel was placed at the butt end of the rod. Charles F. Orvis invented the first ventilated spool fly reel in 1874 and patented it that year. Reels made by Jonathan Meek and Edward Vom Hofe are prized. Theirs, and indeed most of the antique reels available, date from the 1880s. The usual metals employed were brass and nickel plate, but others are known, and some reels have a silver or gold finish. They quite often carry the name of the manufacturer and a patent date.

FLIES. The lure dressed as an insect, which is called a fly, has an especially American history. The first American to tie flies in true imitation of a living insect and sell them commercially was Sarah McBride, in the middle nineteenth century. A more famous name is that of Mary Orvis Marbury,

the daughter of Charles F. Orvis, who was a notable tier. She tied to standard patterns that are still used, but her particular accomplishment was to set forth the whole system of fly-tying in a classic book, *Favorite Flies and Their Histories*, which was first published in 1892.

A fly book of the late nineteenth century was generally made of calf, pigskin, or some other leather and had parchment leaves on which the flies were hooked. The importance and value of flies depends on the skill of the tier. A number of printed books contain actual flies inserted either in the text or in an accompanying volume. These are among the very rare items that combine the literature of a sport with its antiques. The most famous author whose works contain actual flies is Frederic M. Halford, who published a long series of angling books between about 1890 and 1910. Such books are occasionally issued today, generally privately printed.

Because angling often requires so much equipment, a great number of categories of well-made antique items can be collected, and today may be bought at quite reasonable prices—mostly at country auctions. They include, to name only a few:

Fishermen and other sportsmen often adorn their caps or hats with small pins. The habit derives remotely from the medieval custom of pinning a cast-lead badge of a certain design on a religious pilgrim's cap, to indicate that he had visited a particular shrine. For example, a badge showing spiked wheels indicated a visit to a shrine of St. Catherine, who was said to have been martyred on a burning wheel. Several sports are represented on these hat ornaments and pins from Germany, Switzerland, and Austria. Shooting is indicated by the gun pins with various birds and animals shown, including the mountain goat and squirrel, and mountaineering in those with axes, ropes, and boots. The large circular pin at the bottom shows a very ancient huntsman's insignia, St. Hubert's stag with a gold cross above its antlers. The shield-shaped pins are the arms of various towns in Central Europe, or they show peaks and their altitudes. That from the Zugspitze, the highest peak in West Germany, displays ski equipment. Such ornaments are modestly priced and widely collected. Collection of James F. Carr, New York

The canoe has been used for travel by the Indian tribes of North America for centuries; in modern times canoeing has become a sport as well as a mode of transportation, especially on hunting and fishing trips. The form of a canoe has changed very little from that described by the early explorers of North America. The Indian construction material was generally birchbark, but the white man has used canvas, aluminum, and fiberglass. This sixteen-foot canoe constructed of chestnut wood was photographed in Fredericton, New Brunswick, Canada, where it was used for travel. Other boats, such as kayaks, are also collectible and are becoming increasingly popular. Dr. Dustan Osborn, Halifax

Little bells attached to lines, which tinkle
    when the fish bite
Creels (wicker baskets to hold a catch)
Brass frames (for drying linen lines)
Fish spears
Tackle boxes (some elaborately fitted)

An important source of information about and illustration of antique fishing equipment is *Great Fishing Tackle Catalogs of the Golden Age*, edited by Samuel Melner and Hermann Kessler (Crown, 1972), which reprints more than forty catalogues of fishing equipment originally issued between 1839 and 1931. The descriptions and illustrations are invaluable in assisting the angling collector in identifying his angling antiques.

SPORTING GUNS

The crossbow, used in Europe for hunting and military purposes alike from at least the thirteenth century, was the direct ancestor of the sporting gun. It was the final development of the bow and arrow, shooting heavier arrows or even stones. The crossbow was easier to aim and to bend. It was wound by a "cric," a mechanical device using a cog and rack. Before the sixteenth century it was made of layers of whalebone, sinew, and wood. In that century, however, the crossbow came to be formed of an arc of steel with a stock of bone or ivory. Sometimes the stocks were very richly ornamented and, like so many examples of arms and armor, are true works of art valued today for their craftsmanship. Much scholarship has understandably been devoted to the study of these arms.

From the collector's point of view it is surprising that bows and arrows, despite their universal use for centuries, are so extremely rare. According to the arms catalogue of the Metropolitan Museum, "it is a curious fact that not a single specimen of

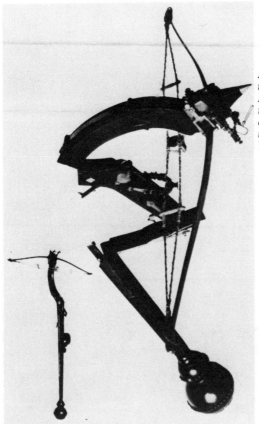

A collapsible crossbow in the Hofjagdkammer *in the Hofburg Palace, Vienna, made in Northern Italy, belonged to the Holy Roman Emperor Ferdinand II, who reigned between 1619 and 1637. The crossbow, direct ancestor of the gun, was used in war and in hunting.* Austrian Information Service, New York

the early English longbow . . . appears to have survived." Each auction season, however, a few crossbows reach the salesrooms, and dealers in arms and armor can usually supply a sixteenth- or seventeenth-century example. They are not, of course, cheap, although on the whole a fine crossbow of that era costs less than a fine early gun. Two typical prices at London sales in the early 1970s were a German crossbow dated 1552, which sold for $2,000, and a fine late-sixteenth-century example, also German, with its original cording of leather and inlaid with engraved horn and brass, which sold for $5,000.

The crossbow was superseded by the gun only very slowly; it is a mistake to think of the introduction of gunpowder into Europe as a sudden revolution. The acceptance of the gun using powder was slow—the crossbow continued to be used along with the gun for several centuries. Gunpowder was not manufactured in England, for example,

until the reign of Elizabeth I, in the late sixteenth century. There was a distinct prejudice against the new weapon that lasted for generations, especially among rank and file military, who clung to their longbows and crossbows, and even among sportsmen, who had their heavy crossbows for big game and light ones for birds and rabbits. The late Bashford Dean, a noted expert on arms and armor, suggested astutely that in a religious age the firing of gunpowder perhaps "savoured of witchcraft and the sulphurs of Satan."

First the matchlock gun, then innumerable other varieties, finally overtook the crossbow in the sixteenth century. The matchlock required tinder in rope form (the "match") to be ignited in the "lock" to fire the gun. The match was pushed down squarely upon the small pan of powder, which led into the gun barrel by a mechanism called the "serpentine." Matchlocks were used for fowling. Since the gun was

Maximilian Wenger was gunsmith to two Holy Roman Emperors, working first in Prague, then in Vienna, in the first half of the seventeenth century. This wheel-lock hunting rifle with inlaid stock is from his hand; it was made about 1630. Austrian Information Service, New York

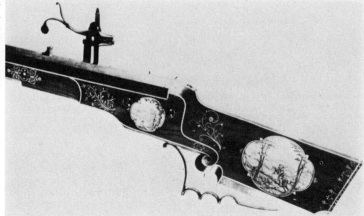

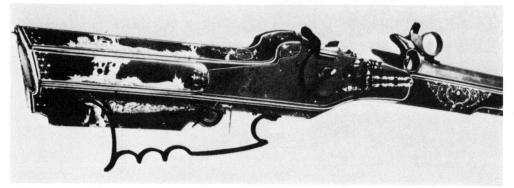

The career of Wenger coincided with the highest period of skill in decorating hunting guns. This wheel lock is enriched with inlays of mother-of-pearl and ivory. Austrian Information Service, New York

slow and heavy and not very accurate the birds had to be shot sitting, which of course required stalking them with great ingenuity.

The old laws and customs regarding the pursuit of game and poaching remained in force even when the weapons changed from bows and arrows to guns. At first, in most countries, guns were allowed to persons not of noble birth for practice, shooting matches, and military service only. The lower classes were forbidden to kill birds or game with the arms; only the nobles were supposed to use their matchlocks for hunting. Such laws were naturally difficult to enforce, and it is

certain that commoners took birds (the "pot shot") with the guns issued to them for practice. The matchlock, incidentally, has a long history in America; it was the gun carried by the Pilgrims. Matchlocks are quite rare on today's collectors' market.

The wheel-lock gun was invented in the early sixteenth century. The brilliant period of its manufacture was 1530–1690. The "match" was discarded in its design and the principle of flint and steel introduced. The flint remained stationary and the steel spun around in the form of a wheel to light it and fire the barrel. The most beautifully dec-

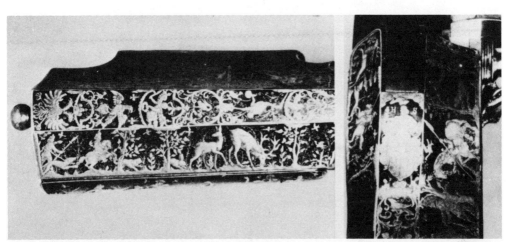

Hans Schmidt of Ferlach in the province of Carinthia, Austria, made this hunting wheel-lock gun, so heavily decorated with silver that it is known as "the silver rifle," for an Austrian prince in the seventeenth century. Note the decoration of hunting scenes. Austrian Information Service, New York

orated guns ever made date from this period, the chief centers of gunsmithing being Italy, France, Germany, and Austria.

At the same time the rifling of barrels was introduced. The inner surface of the gun barrel is cut, in this process, by spiral grooves that give the bullet rotary motion. Both the wheel lock and the rifling were important developments for the sportsman: the wheel lock could be carried more easily than the matchlock since it had no burning match, and rifling gave the gun greater accuracy at long range. Many types of wheel-lock guns were made for sporting, fowling pieces and boar guns among them.

The superb sixteenth- and seventeenth-century wheel-lock guns have always been collected. Even at the time of their manufacture they were highly esteemed, and it is well known that many were intended for show as well as service. Highly decorated examples are found in all the great museums that collect arms, and numerous guns also

come on the market even today. Their price can range up to many thousands of dollars, depending on the maker (many are signed or identifiable as to gunsmith) and the amount and value of the decoration on the stock.

The flintlock, the next great stage in gun development, became popular by the middle of the seventeenth century. In the flintlock a piece of flint strikes against steel and produces sparks that ignite the priming. One variety of the flintlock, the snaphaunce, has a somewhat different firing action but uses flint and steel. Many fine flintlock sporting guns were made. The invention also was a great encouragement for sport because flintlock fowling pieces were lighter and had a light butt that fit well onto the shooter's shoulder and cheek and greatly increased the accuracy of his aim. This made it possible to shoot flying birds, and shooting from horseback became a great sport among the nobility who were allowed to kill game.

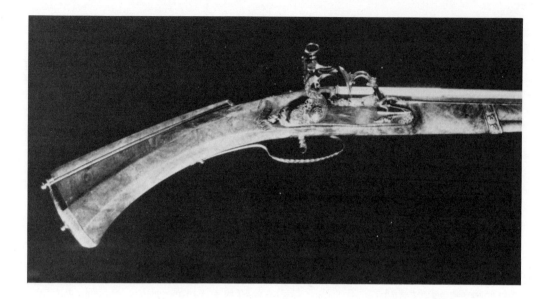

Giovanni Battista I. Francino was the maker of this snaphaunce carbine, now in the armory at Vienna. It is dated Brescia, 1650, and also signed by two other gunsmiths. Brescia was famous for its arms industry. Austrian Information Service, New York

Collectors especially associate the flintlock gun with a dynasty of French gunsmiths named le Bourgeoys. The most expensive gun ever sold at auction was made by a member of this family, Pierre le Bourgeoys. It is a flintlock fowling piece, commissioned by King Louis XIII of France about 1615, and sold at auction in London in 1972 for $312,500. It is now in the Metropolitan Museum of Art, New York.

Louis XIII was one of the most dedicated, not to say fanatical, hunters of his time, spending hours every day in the saddle. He preferred to hunt in the open country in a simple manner. The memoirist Duc de Saint-Simon said he did without "the multitude of huntsmen, hounds, relays, and other complications" later added by his son Louis XIV. Saint-Simon's father was one of the king's pages. He, a clever boy, observed the king's impatience at the delay caused by changing horses during long stag runs and got the idea of bringing a fresh horse nose to tail with the one the king was riding so that the king, who was athletic, could swing from one to the other and not lose the pace. Young Saint-Simon's bright idea made him a favorite of the king and eventually brought him wealth and rank.

Louis XIII, like most sportsmen of his day, hunted whatever game came his way, although the stag was always the prime object. Le Bourgeoys's gun was probably used by the king to shoot rabbits and other small game. It bore the inventory number 134 of the royal Cabinet d'Armes. This was the armory where the king, who was of a melancholic disposition, used to spend hours alone, dismantling, cleaning, and reassembling his many guns.

Flintlocks of the eighteenth century survive in great numbers. Depending on condition and decoration, they may sell from a few hundred dollars to as many thousands. Guns that have had some parts replaced are naturally less desirable. Examples of the work of makers of nearly every European country are to be found represented in collections. Generally speaking, pistols sell for more than long guns. The most elaborate decoration was lavished on them.

By the eighteenth century, shooting game had become a recognized sport. All ranks began to go after game birds, the nobles losing interest in the bigger game or, rather, finding it more scarce. As noted earlier, this is the period when staghunting declined and fox hunting (in England, at least) began to take its place. Fowling pieces were manufactured on a large scale. As Harold Peterson, a noted expert, has written, "the long fowler was the very first of a host of specialized sporting arms that have appeared ever since." Some of these fowlers were five to six feet long. Brought to America by the English, the fowler developed many regional variations.

Profound differences between field sports in England and Europe emerged in the eighteenth century. The Europeans liked a large, well-organized shooting party and the battue (the killing of driven game). The sporting writer Robert Surtees described the English sportsman's way:

A man goes out with his dogs and gun, just as he would with his walking stick; roves the fields, looks at his stock or his drains, or his turnips, or the coming corn; goes just as fancy prompts him, or his dog inclines to his game; if he gets his two or three brace of birds, well and good, if not, he gets healthy exercise, and the birds are there for another day.

In 1807 the Reverend Alexander John Forsyth, who had a parish in Aberdeenshire, Scotland, and was an ardent seeker of wildfowl in its waters, invented and patented percussion ignition for a gun. This involved several technical changes from the flintlock, but the main advantage of the new gun was its speed in firing, which naturally appealed to sportsmen. By 1830 percussion had almost entirely taken the place of the flintlock. In the final years of the flintlock in England, however, a family of gunsmiths

Queen Victoria gave this double-barreled 12-bore gun made by Alexander Henry of Edinburgh to John Brown, her famous and controversial Scottish servant, for Christmas in 1873. Henry was one of the foremost British gunsmiths of the nineteenth century, and the gun and its case with accouterments are fine examples of the best work of the time. There is a presentation inscription from the Queen to Brown on the gold escutcheon set in the stock. Howard Ricketts Limited, London

called Manton built sporting guns that have become famous among sportsmen and collectors.

John Manton went into business as a gunmaker in 1782, and Joseph, his younger brother, started his firm in 1789. The Manton guns and those of contemporary makers came in mahogany cases lined with green baize and holding a huge amount of accouterment such as powder flask, wadcutter, instruments for cleaning, spare parts, and so on. The entire ensemble, as beautifully made as the guns themselves, continues to tempt gun collectors. Cases are more commonly associated with dueling pistols than with sporting guns, but the latter are occasionally to be found in their cases.

Percussion gunmakers of note include James Purdey, Samuel and Charles Smith, Charles Lancaster, Rigby, and Joseph Lang. All made specialized sporting guns, and their products are all collected today.

After 1850 a whole series of inventions improved the sporting gun. These include

The leather case of the John Brown gun is stamped with the owner's name. "H.M.P. Attendant" means "Her Majesty's Personal Attendant," the rank created for Brown in the royal household. Howard Ricketts Limited, London

the breech-loading gun, the center-fire cartridge, and the hammer gun. Three firms —Lancaster, Lang, and Purdey—continued to make guns, using the new devices; among other makers of what are now called "modern sporting guns" are Holland & Holland, Dickson, Churchill, Boss, and Westley Richards. Many of these are in business today.

The new refinements and skilled makers produced the fine guns needed in the late nineteenth century. It was a great age of shooting when sportsmen's estates had beaters and gamekeepers whose entire work was geared to producing the largest possible bags. Some of these have been mentioned earlier. A guest at the Duke of Devonshire's hunting box noted in 1872 that "the swarms of grouse killed become a perplexity in the disposing of them: 400 brace today."

This game did not, of course, go begging: it was an important source of fresh meat for the upper classes, their staffs, tenantry, and guests. Enormous quantities of game were shot, but enormous quantities were consumed. Venison, woodcock, pheasant, and ptarmigan were much more common on dinner tables then than now. King Edward VII, for example, especially liked pheasant that had been stuffed with snipe or woodcock stuffed in turn with truffles, as one dish at dinner.

One writer has described this kind of shooting as "a quasi-military operation," and like a military operation it had its uniforms, which became increasingly elaborate in the nineteenth century and assumed the specialization that one sees today in going through catalogues of L. L. Bean, Orvis, and Abercrombie & Fitch. The origin of special hunting clothes is probably Germanic. By the nineteenth century a German *Jagd-Partie* wore gray-green suits faced with dark green, with a green Tyrolese hat decorated with a blackcock's tail, high boots, a green sling for the gun, and a game bag with a green tassel. Lord Frederick Hamilton, who went on shooting parties in Germany in the 1870s, remarked that the tasseled game bag was considered an "absolute essential concomitant to a *Jagd-Partie*." He commented that "the guns all looked like the chorus in *Der Freischütz*, and I expected them to break at any moment into the 'Huntsmen's Chorus.' " This kind of costume persisted in Germany into the present century. The Nazi Marshal Hermann Goering, who, after Hitler took power, became "Reich Master of the Hunt," always wore a special hunt uniform consisting of a white silk shirt with puffed sleeves over which he wore a sleeveless leather-belted jacket.

Some very unusual guns for sportsmen were made in this era. Among them was the "punt gun," which is a smoothbore fowling piece fired from a small boat called a punt. It was used especially for waterfowl and could down between twenty and forty birds at a single shot. Many sportsmen understandably abhorred this slaughter; the gun was outlawed in the United States in 1916. Single-barreled "big game pistols" were made for use in the Far East and Africa. One of these was the so-called howdah pistol, which was used to finish off large game after it had been wounded with a long smoothbore. The famous muzzle-loading "elephant guns" were another type. These big game rifles were very large arms, probably the largest ever made except some military pieces.

"Modern sporting guns" are widely collected, sometimes for actual use and sometimes for their antique value. The term is used to cover guns made since about 1850, which are also referred to as "vintage" guns in the trade. A sidelock ejector 12-bore sporting shotgun made by J. Purdey or a similar Holland and Holland can easily sell for $3,000 up. Many built-to-order British guns being made today cost more.

American guns of great interest to the collector include the Kentucky rifle, which goes back as far as the eighteenth century, and the "Plains rifle," which had a shortened barrel for carrying on horseback and was made in various calibers, including .45

A fine example of the modern sporting gun, a double-barreled 12-bore sidelock hammerless ejector model built by Henry Aitken, which sold in 1973 for $2,100. Phillips Auctioneers, London

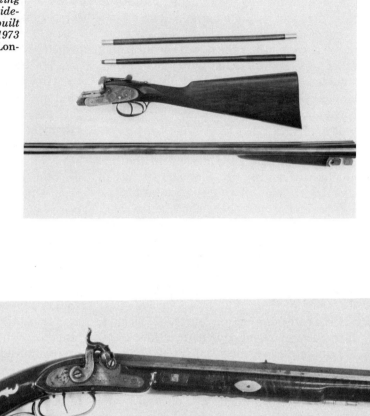

The so-called "Plains rifle," which played a great role in hunting in the western United States. Its name is said to have come from a misunderstanding of "plain rifle," originally meaning an unornamented one. Kit Carson, the celebrated trapper, guide, and Indian agent, was presented with this .36 half-stock Plains rifle "by his friends in Las Vegas, N.M. July 14, 1852," as the stock is inscribed. It was sold at auction in 1974 for $1,300. Sotheby Park Bernet Los Angeles

to .55 for big game. In general, however, there are fewer American guns of sporting interest. A major source of information about them has recently become available to the collector in the reprinted old trade catalogues of gun manufacturers and retailers. These give facts about and pictorial representation of guns and gun equipment that are now highly collectible. Among others, the 1914 Winchester gun catalogue has been reprinted, the 1916 Remington Arms, and the 1914 G & L Sporting Goods Store.

Powder horns and flasks were necessary

Dr. William H. Keller, an American, was personal physician to President Porfirio Díaz of Mexico, who had seven terms in office between 1877 and 1911. Dr. Keller is shown here on various hunting expeditions in Mexico—with game taken in the two photographs at left, in studio shots in hunting poses at right. His favorite hunting dog is shown with him in the farthest right photograph. When the dog died, this photograph was sent to Paris and a French artist made and cast the bronze sculpture shown at left. Collection of James F. Carr, New York

Percival Rousseau, an American artist (died 1937) who was an active sportsman himself, is noted for his portrayal of hunting dogs. He once attempted the unpromising project of establishing fox hunting in the state of Texas. This is his Two Hunting Dogs in a Clearing *(1919). Oil on canvas, 23 x 29 inches. Graham Gallery, New York*

In the past, owners of hunting dogs often spent lavishly on fine collars for their animals. In medieval tapestries of hunting scenes dogs are shown wearing broad collars richly mounted in metal and decorated with the names or initials or arms of their masters. In some parts of Central Europe, however, the dogs were branded with the initials or devices of their owners. In Saxony, the elector's dogs were branded with the crossed swords device, the same used on Meissen porcelain. From a somewhat later period comes this fine brass collar for a dog, possibly a small mastiff or a bull terrier. Its inside diameter is six inches, and it is two inches deep. The engraving is the name of the dog's owner, Mrs. B. Pye Benet of Bath. Rupert Gentle

Hunters have always enjoyed being depicted with their game. In ancient times they were painted. In the nineteenth century, the camera came to record exploits. This is Armand, Duc de Riche-lieu, who died in 1880, and a fine stag, probably taken near his home, the Château de Haut-Buisson, France. Collection of James F. Carr, New York

Several members of the British royal family have been noted shots, especially King George V. His eldest son, Edward VIII, later Duke of Windsor, excelled at shooting and many other sports, including polo. He appears here with his Duchess (at left) at a shooting party in South Carolina. Photograph loaned by James F. Carr, New York

Leopold V of Austria is portrayed on a silver powder flask, which he commissioned from Hans Schmidt of Ferlach. Mid-seventeenth century. Austrian Information Service, New York

concomitants to the gun for several centuries. Like hunting horns, powder horns took their name from the earliest material used in making them—the horns of cattle, ibex, deer, chamois, and other animals. The horn was often mounted in metal and there was always a wooden or metal plug or stopper at the smaller end to be used in releasing the gunpowder, and usually a cap at the larger end also. Later wood, ivory, various metals (brass, copper, pewter, tin), and hardened leather were used, but the horn shape was preserved. Sometimes the metal was leather covered.

The horn was first boiled and the core removed. It was then scraped clean and the smaller end drilled and fitted with the plug. Horn is easily engraved or even scratched with designs, and many powder horns are richly decorated. Many, perhaps most, European and American powder horns have coats of arms, mottoes, views, flags, and even maps engraved on them. It is not at all uncommon for them to be dated. One

might almost say that the unengraved powder horn is a rarity. Those with military reference, especially of American origin, have always been the most sought by collectors in this country. Those with hunting scenes are equally attractive and generally much cheaper. True horns are much more expensive than the metal flasks. Currently (1975) good horns of the nineteenth century with routine decoration sell between $100 and $200; metal flasks are perhaps half those prices.

In addition to the gun cases containing materials for cleaning and repairing, which have accompanied new guns since the early nineteenth century, a variety of gun cases, gun chests, suitcases, and other storage and shipping containers for firearms has been manufactured during the last century. Some of these have been made of fine woods, others of leather or canvas. The metal plaques or paper labels found on many of these cases supply important information to the gun collector. The cases for carrying

The Wild Boar Hunt *by the seventeenth-century animal painter Frans Snyders, once in the Dresden Gallery, shows how spears have always been used in hunting boar. These hunters are on foot, but when the hunters are mounted the sport is known as pigsticking.*

the "battery" for big-game hunting during the golden age of the sport, in the late nineteenth century, when trips might last for months or even years, are especially handsome.

HUNTING SWORDS AND KNIVES

The hunting sword is a shorter and lighter sword than that used for military purposes. The blade is usually straight or very slightly curved. European hunting swords date back to the Middle Ages, but they were made through the nineteenth century. They were used not only to dispatch a wounded animal, but to cut up the game after the kill. In many places, this was a time of great ceremony. The hilts of the swords, like those of military or court swords, were made of ivory, gilded bronze, or even silver. The sheath might also serve as a *trousse* (a tool kit), containing knives and forks and sometimes special instruments to aid in cutting up the game. In the eighteenth and nineteenth centuries as the habit of regularly wearing a military or court sword disappeared, some men wore the short hunting sword as stylish accompaniment to their dress.

Some hunting swords were made in colonial and federal America. A silver-mounted hunting sword by John Bailey of Fishkill, New York, which belonged to General George Washington, is still preserved in the United States National Museum, Washington.

Swords long constituted an indispensable part of the huntsman's equipment. These examples made in Northern Italy in the mid-seventeenth century are shown with their scabbards. Austrian Information Service, New York

An eighteenth-century hunting sword that was sold in 1974 for $100. The pommel and grip are brass; the length is 25 inches. The place of origin is unknown. Sotheby Parke Bernet Los Angeles

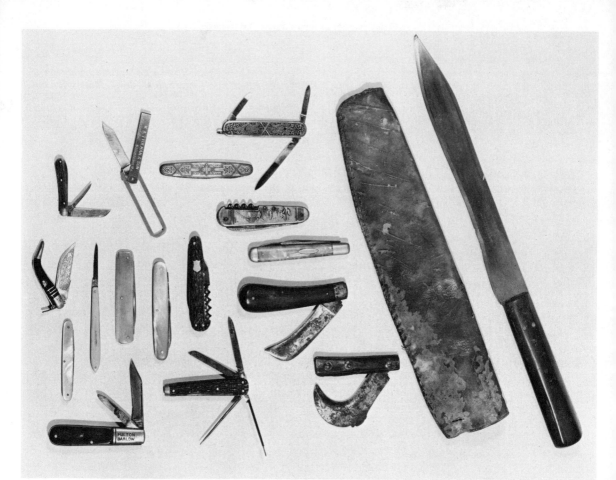

A large gathering of hunting, fishing, and other knives. The large knife at right has a 9¾-inch blade. Made by J. Russell & Co. and patented in 1872, it belonged to General David J. Brainard and was used by him while on military service in the Indian fighting in the Dakotas in the 1870s. From 1881 to 1884 he was a member of the Greely Arctic Expedition; he and a companion reached the farthest northern point that had been reached to that time. He carried this knife with him. The sheath is Plains rawhide, possibly deer or antelope. At the lower left is a Fulton Barlow knife carried by plainsmen and many other American men of the mid-nineteenth century. It is known that Abraham Lincoln owned a Barlow. Among the other knives, which are mostly American with a few English, are examples with handles of bone, horn, stainless steel, hardwood, ivory, damascened steel, ebony, and brass. The third from the top in the center is decorated with fishing scenes and signed "Depose." Collection of James F. Carr, New York

Opposite page
The great halls of European castles have always displayed the armories of the owners and usually a variety of animal trophies. Many types of arms, armor, military and hunting costume, banners, heads, and antlers line the arms hall at Schloss Langenburg, home of His Serene Highness Prince Kraft zu Hohenlohe-Langenburg, in West Germany, shown as it is today. German Information Center, New York

Hunting swords are comparatively expensive on today's market, but hunting knives, which have been made in a profusion of types (see the illustration), are plentiful, interestingly varied, and generally inexpensive. Pocketknives with a single blade, multiple blades, various implements such as files, and accouterments such as compasses in their cases are attracting more and more attention from collectors. The cases, as the illustration shows, can be made of dozens of different substances. There are even gold, silver, and jeweled cases. A great many nineteenth-century American knives of unusual design were patented, and consequently they very often bear the name of the manufacturing company and a patent registration date, which makes them of greater interest to the collector. Among especially famous company names are Barlow, Waldeman, Camillus Cutlery, and Remington Arms. Knives made by the last named are much sought by collectors today and probably command the highest prices. Although good case and pocketknives, unless of unusual design, are selling for under $25, Remington knives can often bring as much as $100.

Among European manufacturers of the nineteenth and twentieth centuries, Solingen of Germany was noted for knives. Many of these are hunting knives, and there is one variety known as the "Royal Buffalo Skinner." Many Solingen knives,

which are marked with the company's name, are still modestly priced today, selling for under $25.

AMERICAN BIRD DECOYS

The bird decoy is a carved figure, usually in the form of a waterfowl or shorebird, used to lure live birds within shooting range. It is a specifically American object, and one of the most charming and ardently collected antiques of sport.

Very few decoys are really "antique" by the current definition, since they are not yet one hundred years old. Colonial Americans stuffed the skins of dead birds with rushes and floated them on the water to attract flocks; a few crude carved and painted decoys are said to date to about 1850, but the birds sought by collectors today were mostly made after 1870. The golden age of decoy carving was the forty-year period from about 1880 to the First World War.

Millions of wildfowl and shorebirds were shot during that era, not primarily for sport but for food. A glance at almost any dinner menu shows how popular dishes like canvasback duck were, with Americans in the "Gilded Age." Many of the best shooting grounds were near the cities where the demand existed. Jamaica Bay in New York City, for example, was a prime ground, and the birds taken there were sold in the city's markets by men who made a living supplying the hotels and restaurants. William J. Mackey, Jr., who was the foremost scholar and collector of American bird decoys, wrote of this period: "The greatest waterfowl hunt in the history of the world had begun and was continued until 1918, when the passage of sane laws put an end to the slaughter."

Regional style is very important in the making of decoys. There were two principal areas where the birds were created—the Atlantic coast from Massachusetts to the Carolinas, and the inland region between St. Louis and Chicago. Within these large areas were numerous smaller ones, each depicting the native birds in its own style. Careful study has distinguished many differences in the work of the various areas. The finest decoys are generally from the Middle Atlantic states.

Decoys are usually divided into two types —the floating (ducks and geese principally), which are held in place on the water by a lead weight attached to a line, and "stick-ups" or stationary birds (mostly shorebirds), which are flat and put down on stakes on land or in shallow water. These were sawed and chiseled from thick board. Pine was the earliest wood used, but the most common are cedar or white juniper. Sometimes wood from wrecked ships was carved, and it might be a much more exotic variety. Some decoys were made from cork.

The best bird decoys were (and are) carved, and there have been thousands of carvers, but decoys were (and are) also made in factories, then finished and painted by hand. Many of these factory productions are quite as valid collectors' items as the carved birds, displaying a high degree of skill.

The collecting of bird decoys offers much scope for the collector, as it is not a simple field. Duck decoys alone are an entire area of specialization: there are about twenty species of native ducks, and the drake and duck (the female) have different plumage, so there is a great variety to collect. There are also regional differences in carving and of course different carvers. The same is true of geese and of other species. Shorebird decoys are rarer than wildfowl, but at least nineteen varieties of them are known, including sandpipers, snipe, plovers, and curlews. And there are decoys for swans, herons, loons, crows, owls, and gulls as well.

Among the most famous decoy carvers, whose works command hundreds and sometimes thousands of dollars, are (proceeding down the Atlantic coast):

Elmer Crowell (Massachusetts)
Ben Holmes (Connecticut)

Albert Laing (Connecticut)
Charles "Shang" Wheeler (Connecticut)
Harry Shourdes (New Jersey)
Henry Grant (New Jersey)
Lloyd Parker (New Jersey)
Ira Hudson (Virginia)
Nathan Cobb (Virginia)
Lee and Lem Dudley (Carolinas)

Factories that have produced fine decoys include:

Dodge Decoy Factory
Mason's Decoy Company
William E. Pratt Manufacturing
    Company
Stevens Decoy Factory
C. V. Wells Factory
Wildfowler Decoys, Inc.

The best-known collection of bird decoys was that of William J. Mackey, Jr., quoted above. He was the author of the standard *American Bird Decoys*. At the time of his death in 1972, he had between two thousand six hundred and three thousand shorebird and waterfowl decoys in his collection. In fact, he had collected in such depth that he even had a group of the baskets used to carry decoys to the shooting areas. The Mackey Collection was sold in a series of sales in 1973/4. At the time, it was considered "the largest and most important decoy collection ever formed." In addition to the usual woods, Mackey owned decoys made of iron, cardboard, canvas, tin, and papier-mâché. He had begun his collecting in the 1930s, when there was little if any interest in such a humble American art, and so he had unrivaled opportunities to gather rare birds.

At the sales there were two high points. The highest price was paid for a Hudsonian curlew carved by William Bowman—it sold for $10,500. A great blue heron carved by Elmer Crowell sold for $8,000.

4

GAME TROPHIES

Collecting game trophies is a field in which relatively small amounts of money can be laid out to great advantage today. Mounted heads that are fine examples of animal life as well as of the taxidermist's expert work and antlers of all variety and number of points are often sold for very small sums indeed. The reason is, quite simply, that trophies, especially of the big-game animals, are usually considered personal items; bagging them has been an individual's achievement, and ownership of the trophy is his symbol. Many collectors who have been successful hunters do not care to buy trophies that have been taken by other hunters.

The pride of ownership in a fine animal trophy was explained many years ago by Clive Phillipps-Wolley, a fine shot and the editor of the Badminton Library volume on hunting:

More than all the pleasures which the rich man feels as he surveys his Murillos or his Raphaels are the hunter's, as his eyes wander over his antlered walls. *He* shot the beasts whose spoils are round him, and in the doing of it scenes were graven on his memory which never can be effaced.

The fact that most hunters prefer trophies of their own bagging has never prevented the purchase of trophies either by persons who were hunters themselves but failed to bag the desired specimens, or by people who simply wanted a striking decoration for a hall or den, or by collectors of natural history specimens. And, of course, the fine stuffed specimens on display in museums all over the world were obtained by big-game hunters. Some of these hunters were employed by the museums at the time the game was taken; other specimens were bought by museums at sales of trophies.

During the most active days of big-game hunting, local hunters in many parts of the world offered to sell the animals they had taken, to visiting big-game hunters who had missed their shots, so to speak. In parts of Canada, which was a great source of fine heads and horns, traders used to have printed price lists of trophies according to the number of inches they measured round the base or the length and span of the antlers.

Not only the shooting of the game but the preparation of the trophies was taken very seriously in the golden age of big game hunting, from the 1880s to the Second World War. Books written to help hunters who were going on safari in the great game regions like Eastern Africa used to suggest that one of the hunters be adept at photography, so that any specimen taken could be photographed as a guide to the taxidermist when he was presented with the head, horns, and skin to prepare the specimen for display. Game taken was packed in salt and alum or even "pickled" in brine or chemicals to keep it until the hunter returned to the place where expert taxidermy was available, usually London. The time gap was of course likely to be much longer in the nineteenth century than it became in the twentieth. Most of the hunters' books give detailed instruction for skinning the animal, preserving the mountable parts, and caring for them in transit.

Big game trophies were more often sold at auction in the nineteenth century than today. A famous early sale was that of trophies shot by the big game hunter Roualeyn Gordon-Cumming, who hunted in South Africa from 1843 to 1848 and wrote a best-selling book on his experiences, *Five Years of a Hunter's Life* (1850). He exhibited his trophies at the Great Exhibition at the Crystal Palace in 1851 and later at his private museum in his native Scotland. In 1866, after his death, Gordon-Cumming's trophies were sold at auction, accompanied by his own catalogue descriptions. They included the skulls, tusks, tails, teeth, and feet of elephants, the skulls and horns of the rhinoceros, giraffe heads, and the skulls of buffalo, and attracted much public attention. Among the principal bidders was P. T. Barnum, who displayed his acquisitions to the public in his famous "museum."

Today, the larger auction houses seldom have sales of trophies, skins (except as "furs"), or antlers. It was therefore unusual when, in February 1973, the Los Angeles branch of the Sotheby Parke Bernet auction house sold the large trophy collection formed by John Quincy Adams IV, who had died in 1959. The great-great-grandson of the sixth president of the United States, Adams made more than thirty-five trips to Alaska in his attempt to secure as perfect a collection of North American wildlife as possible, to preserve specimens for posterity; he had over one hundred stuffed animals and birds. (This sale will be referred to several times.) The most common source for buying a head, antlers, or an entire mounted animal is now the country auction. The Victorian and Edwardian house often had sufficient space to display a pair of fine antlers, an unusual stuffed bird, or a record fish.

The art of taxidermy no longer flourishes. Even in the largest cities, such as New York, most of the remaining firms merely rent older specimens to television and movie studios. The mounting that is done today is, as most advertise, of "un-endangered species only." Conservation laws have almost entirely destroyed this profession. It is unlikely that many items of collectors'

More than 100 animal and bird trophies were collected by the naturalist and sportsman John Quincy Adams IV. Shown here is his living room. The collection was sold at auction in Los Angeles in February 1973. Sotheby Parke Bernet Los Angeles

interest will be produced again.*

The commonest animal trophy is the antlers of deer, preserved with or without the head. There is no reason to suppose that they will soon become rare, even with the proliferation of conservation laws. Many antlers are simply picked up because deer shed their antlers annually. There are still a great many antlered animals shot. In 1974, it was estimated that the state of Wyoming had an elk herd of about 100,000 animals of which about 20,000 were "harvested," as hunters say now, each season. And there were large numbers of the animals in Montana, Idaho, and Colorado. The family *Cervidae* is found in most parts of the world, and antlers, which are solid bony outgrowths of the skull, develop in the males of most species.

Some of the great houses in Europe built since medieval times and a few in America built in the nineteenth or the early twentieth century show a perfect forest of antlers on their walls as decoration and as memorials of the chase. Many of these carry a plaque —especially if they are of spectacular size— giving the date the animal was shot and the name of the hunter.

* The United States Endangered Species Act of 1973, which went into operation on 28 December 1973, was aimed not only at living animals but also antiques derived from endangered species. These antiques include an immense array of objects, such as the feathers of various birds found in historic costumes and fans, stuffed birds and animals, crocodile pocketbooks, pianos with ivory keys, some Japanese netsuke because they are made of whale ivory; also buggy whips, umbrellas, and corset stays using whalebone in their construction, furniture with tortoiseshell insets, and scrimshaw. Zealous federal agents seized a number of antique objects from dealers, including large quantities of scrimshaw regardless of the fact that most of it had been made from whalebone over a century earlier. At the time of writing (1974), attempts are being made by the antique trade and collectors to have the Act modified to allow continued commerce in old objects of animal origin, which the Act calls broadly "parts and products of fish or wildlife."

In Central Europe, where traditionally deer were shot as driven game rather than stalked, bags and the consequent accumulation of antlers reached mammoth proportions. The memoirs of Daisy, Princess of Pless, an English girl who married one of the wealthiest men in the German Empire, with an annual income estimated at about $1,000,000 in present-day terms, give an incomparable picture of the rites of game preservation and hunting practiced in Germany before the First World War. The Princess, a true Englishwoman despite half a lifetime in Germany, considered staghunting by battue "drawing-room shooting," and like most English and American visitors to the continent, disdained it. Nevertheless, she and her husband were obliged to put up tremendous shoots at their Silesian estates for visiting magnates, including Kaiser Wilhelm II. She calculated that each stag shot by a guest cost about $5,000 in today's terms. And at some hunting parties guests shot three or four each. Every year the Kaiser, a devoted hunter despite his crippled arm, gave a monumental cup of fearful Teutonic intricacy to the German citizen who shot the largest stag.

At the estates of the Princes of Schwarzenberg in Bohemia, where sport was pursued for generations on an almost professional scale, a private museum of arms and other hunting equipment was kept, as well as enormous game preserves. One day each week during the hunting season was devoted to a battue of deer and other driven game, and never less than two to three hundred specimens were killed. Great ceremony attended not only the shooting but the "viewing." "The game was laid out in rows," wrote Nora Princess Fugger, a good sportswoman herself, "in the castle yard and was viewed in the evening by the entire hunting party while torches were burning brightly and a band of the Prince's grenadiers sounded an old hunting fanfare."

The taste for decorating halls and other large rooms with horns and heads dates back to medieval times. In Central Europe the taste has persisted. In England, it has had various periods of fashion, most recently at the turn of this century, but such decoration has usually been confined to "trophy rooms." In the United States, antlers have ornamented hunting lodges in both the eastern and western parts of the country. The great hunting lodges built in the Adirondack Mountains late in the last century were especially notable for their decoration with trophies, often including chandeliers made of antlers. Smaller establishments have used them in the "den," a room and an expression that came into vogue only during the nineteenth century and at least until recently had a masculine aura; the earliest use in the Oxford English Dictionary dates to 1771—"a small room in which a *man* can be alone."

An occasional architect or decorator has used trophies in other parts of the house: Stanford White, for example, during his career about the turn of this century, hung antlers in New York drawing rooms in a way most people would now find disconcerting. A splendid example of a house on public view that is decorated throughout with big game trophies shot by the owner is Theodore Roosevelt's famous Sagamore Hill at Oyster Bay, Long Island. A Cape buffalo head dominates the entrance hall. The house has a trophy room containing elk and moose antlers and a pair of enormous elephant tusks from Ethiopia. Even the dinner gong is held by four-foot-high elephant tusks, with a plaque reading "Shot by Theodore Roosevelt in Kenya, Sept. 11, 1909."

The mania for large bags and for showy antlers with great spreads produced staghunters who never knew when to stop. Anne Duchesse d'Uzès, who died in 1933 at the age of eighty-six, was a French sportswoman who in her long hunting career killed more than two thousand stags. Their antlers decorated her hunting lodge in the Forest of Rambouillet near Paris, producing an effect one writer has succinctly described as "grisly." A granddaughter of the Cliquot champagne family, the Duchesse, by all accounts formidable, was able to afford other sports, too; she was a yachtswoman and the first woman in France to have a license to drive a motorcar.

In describing antlers sold on the antique market today, certain terms are used as they are by naturalists in describing the animals. For the collector, the most important to recognize in catalogue descriptions of antlers are these: A *rack* of antlers is a pair. A *tine* is a pointed branch of a deer's antlers. (Antlers are classified by the number of their tines: one says "a rack of ten-tine antlers.") The stem on which these tines grow is called the *beam*.

A *royal rack* of antlers comes from a stag at least eight years old having antlers with at least twelve tines. Antlers *in velvet* means that the rack has the soft, highly vascular, hairy skin that envelops (and nourishes) the antlers of deer during their rapid growth but later peels off or is rubbed off by the stag.

Antlers are generally mounted on wood (often backed with felt) in a shield shape. The dimension given in descriptions is generally the *spread*—i.e., measured tip-to-tip at the widest point of the rack.

Antlers on the collectors' market in the early 1970s realized prices like these:

- Pair of buckhorn heads mounted on shields: $30
- Mounted moose head: $100
- Mule-deer head with antler spread of 25½ inches: $40
- Bull-elk head with fine thirteen-tine rack of antlers, spread of rack 39 inches: $100
- Bull-caribou head, spread of rack 28 inches: $50
- Royal elk rack with spread of 40½ inches, mounted on shield: $100

- Young bull-moose head, mounted,
  with rack of antlers of spread of 67
  inches: $450

The first stuffed specimens of animal life
were probably birds—apparently pets—or
treasured domesticated animals rather than
wild ones. The claim has been made that
the oldest stuffed bird in existence is a
parrot that was the pet of a seventeenth-
century Duchess of Richmond, which is
now (by direction of her will) in Westminster Abbey. At Battle Abbey in England, which is near the site of the Battle of
Hastings, a stuffed black horse said to have
been the identical one that carried William
the Conqueror on that historic day was
proudly shown by the Webster family,
owners of the Abbey during the nineteenth
century. "In reality," sniffed one well-
informed visitor, "the horse in question had
never carried anyone more celebrated than
Sir Godfrey Webster, and then only at a
review."

In taxidermy the fur or feathers of the
dead animal are cleaned, and the skin
mounted on a man-made skeleton. The object, of course, is not only to preserve the
specimen but to make it appear as lifelike
as possible. In earlier times animals were
stuffed with straw; later, they were mounted
on wire netting and papier-mâché. Either
way, they had a tendency to deflate; one
visitor to a British museum remembered
"ghastly limp giraffes."

Readers of Dickens will recall the most
famous taxidermist in literature, Mr. Venus,
"Preserver of Animals and Birds." His main
business was stuffing deceased domestic
pets; it is a stuffed canary that is being
called for when Mr. Wegg visits him. Mr.
Wegg, incidentally, found the smell of the
taxidermist's shop rather overwhelming—
"musty, leathery, feathery, cellary, gluey,
and gummy."

It was not until the late nineteenth century that new research greatly improved
taxidermy. Carl Akeley, an American naturalist, taxidermist, and explorer, devised
a method of mounting that preserved the
actual contours of the specimen with a
plaster mold made as a frame to hold the
skin in position. Most of the fine specimens
seen now in natural history museums and
private collections are made this way.

The subjects of big game trophy hunting
are naturally quite numerous. In the continent of Africa, home of the finest and
most desired specimens, there are more than
one hundred species of game animal. But
big game hunting in Africa has had a rather
short history, although few hunting areas
have inspired more literature and more
motion pictures. The spread of hunting for
sport was closely connected with the spread
of European civilization on the African continent. The legendary early hunters included William Cotton Oswell, who came to
Africa from India as early as 1845 and in
1849 traveled into new regions of Central
America with his friend Dr. David Livingstone. Oswell was an all-round athlete who
was not only a fine hunter but engaged as
well in boxing, racquets, and cricket.

Frederick Courtenay Selous, who first
visited South Africa in 1871, wrote some of
the best books on African hunting. He had
a long career, which ended in 1916, when
he fell in action during the First World War.
Sir Samuel White Baker, who arrived in
Africa in 1860, was one of the great African
explorers of the Nilotic regions. These men
were explorers as well as sportsmen, and
they contributed importantly to the geographical knowledge of the Dark Continent.

The building of the Mombasa-Uganda
railroad in 1896 opened up the interior of
the East African plateau, where there was
the greatest concentration of game animals,
and made visits by sportsmen easier. The
great impetus so far as the American public
was concerned, however, stemmed from the
safari (this is a Swahili word for trip) made
by former president Theodore Roosevelt in
1908.

The end of European government in

The Cape buffalo, noted for its ferocity, is one of the most sought after of African big game trophies. Mr. and Mrs. Edward W. Sheldon bagged this fine specimen in the then Portuguese colony of Mozambique. Edward W. Sheldon

Africa was a major setback for big game hunting and the preservation of wildlife. The protection of animals had made great strides, just before the formation of the new African countries, with the establishment of national parks and game preserves. Much of this was undone during the disorders that followed the forced departure of the Europeans. In the Belgian Congo the natives slaughtered the animals in the famous Prince Albert Parc, and in many parts of the continent poaching for ivory and skins went unchecked. Following the change of government a whole series of laws, many of them contradictory, were passed. In some countries big game hunting was completely forbidden; in others licensed hunters were permitted to shoot in "hunting blocks" that were set aside, with heavy trophy fees levied. In the meantime, many species were declining in numbers. Poaching by natives who smuggled ivory and skins out of the African countries to the Near and Far East, where there is great demand for them, is responsible for much of the decline, but the main cause in Africa, as everywhere, is the relentless pressure of population growth. More land is constantly being brought under cultivation to supply the food needs of the increasing population, and the areas in which wild animals can wander are being reduced.

Most conservation experts, including those who have made studies of East Africa, agree that licensed sport hunting has never been responsible for the extinction of any species because hunters have always tended to shoot the older males that are past breeding, since their well-developed horns and tusks make the best trophies. Nevertheless,

Trophies from Mozambique taken by the Sheldons. They include impala, nyala and sable antelope, warthog, hartebeest, waterbuck, Cape buffalo, bushbuck, and reedbuck. Edward W. Sheldon

the unsettled conditions in the historic game areas of Africa make it unlikely that much hunting, even licensed and fee-paid, will be permitted in the near future. The specimens that exist outside Africa, therefore, are certainly going to become rarer.

Generally, African sportsmen want horned animals as trophies. Outstanding among those of Africa are such species as the greater kudu and the sable antelope. The spiraling horns of the greater kudu are often over sixty inches long. The straight horns of the Arabian oryx, which is found in the Sudan, have been much sought too. The addax (a large, pale-colored antelope) has also been sought for its extremely handsome horns. One shot in the 1960s by Frank C. Hibben, a sportsman and author, was then number two in the world records, the horn length being 41⅜ inches. Hibben also shot an oryx with world-record horns 51¼ inches long.

The "big five" of African hunting, the most desired specimens, are also the most dangerous to hunt. They are the elephant, the rhinoceros, the Cape buffalo, the lion, and the leopard. The first three have horns or tusks; the two cats are valued for their skins. The Cape buffalo, regarded as especially difficult to bag because of its large size and ferocity, sometimes has a horn spread of over fifty inches on both the male and the female. So far as lions go, hunters seek a large male with a long, heavy mane, which can be up to eighteen inches in length.

The search for elephant ivory was a great impetus to big game hunting in Africa. Elephant ivory is, at the same time, one of the most common and one of the most sought trophies of big game, and it has held that rank longer than any other game trophy. Although it is always dangerous to forecast the future rarity of any antique because supplies have a way of showing up just as the announcement is made, ivory does seem destined to become increasingly difficult for the collector to find, since the countries where the ivory-producing animals still exist have nearly all passed laws against its free commerce.

The quantity of ivory produced by one great beast can be astonishing. When "Ahmed," a veritable Methuselah among elephants, died on Mount Marsabit in Kenya in 1974 at an age calculated to be about seventy years, his tusks were ten feet long and weighed a total of 350 pounds. The world-record animal was shot in Uganda. His tusks were *over* ten feet long and weighed 220 pounds *each*.

Chaos in Africa after the withdrawal of most of the European governments in the 1950s, new laws in India, and the worldwide interest in conserving game have combined to reduce the supply of ivory on the market for any purpose. In 1974 it was estimated that about 150,000 elephants remained in

Kenya. Licenses were given to hunters for the killing of 600 per year, but it was thought that native poachers were killing or maiming several thousand a year in their pursuit of ivory. A 93-pound elephant tusk sold that year at a London auction for $2,800, about ten times the price it might have realized only five years before. But five years earlier about 150 tons of ivory were said to pass through the London market; by 1973, the figure was down to only twenty-five tons. The firm of Puddefort, Bowers, and Simonett, one of the oldest ivory firms, stopped dealing in the commodity in 1973.

Typical of the prices realized during the 1970s by big game specimens of African origin and other African trophies are these:

- Small stuffed crocodile, 52 inches
  long: $50
- Pair of African eland horns with
  suede mounts: $400

On the same trip to Mozambique, A. R. Updike shot this waterbuck (Kobus ellipsiprymnus). Edward W. Sheldon

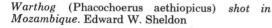
Warthog (Phacochoerus aethiopicus) *shot in Mozambique.* Edward W. Sheldon

- African roan antelope buck, mounted, with horns 26½ inches long: $175
- African zebra skin backed with canvas, 75 inches long from base of tail to base of neck: $150
- Thompson gazelle head with 13-inch horns: $100
- Pair of Cape buffalo horns with spread of 40 inches: $175
- Pair of Arabian oryx horns 29¾ inches long: $90
- Rhinoceros horn, 15 inches long: $25
- Mounted cheetah skin: $50

In India, the prime big game animal has always been the beautiful and elusive tiger, sought in various ways, including the rather horrible one of tying up a live goat as bait. In fact, the history of hunting in India revolves around the dangerous search for the magnificent Indian (or Bengal) tigers;

they are especially famous in the history of Indian princely hunting and in the history of sport in the days of the British raj. Many of the Indian maharajahs were great hunters: one is said to have shot over a thousand tigers in his lifetime. In 1940, counting every small fief ruled by a semi-independent chieftain, there were more than five hundred "native states" in India. Seventy-three of these rulers were considered to be of the first rank and had the title of "Highness" bestowed on them by the British. They were entitled, a very important point, to salutes of more than eleven guns upon arriving for a state visit. Up to the time of Indian independence in 1947 and, indeed, to some extent thereafter, the rites of hunting and shooting on a big scale were kept up among the native princes. They are a fascinating phase of the history of the hunt.

An English visitor who accompanied the Maharajah of Cooch Bejar on his 1891 annual excursion for rhinoceros, buffalo, leopard, and tiger learned to his amazement that the maharajah's staff numbered 473 persons. They included mahouts (elephant drivers), grooms, armorers, tailors, shoemakers, a doctor and dispenser, boatmen, a Viennese conductor and the thirty-five members of his orchestra, cooks, bakers, waiters, and taxidermists to prepare the trophies! Much later, a British journalist described the hunting arrangements of the Maharajah of Dholpur in Rajasthan in northwest India, in the days just before World War II. Each of the many villages in His Highness's domain had a game warden and a telephone. At dawn, each warden telephoned the palace with a report of game sighted around his village. The reports were gathered together by secretaries and summarized, so that at breakfast the maharajah knew just what animals had been seen and in which direction and could plan his day's hunting accordingly.

The Maharajah of Bikaner (another Rajasthan state) was noted for his fabulous grouse shoots. Boys were stationed near the lake where the grouse drank. When the birds approached, the boys scared them off with noise and stones. After two or three days the birds, mad with thirst, were determined to get to the lake. When they came over in clouds, the shooting produced enormous bags.

One of the most interesting ways of hunting was practiced in another Rajasthan state, Jodhpur, where the chinkara (a small deer) was hunted with a trained leopard. The leopard was kept hooded like a falcon until the moment when the quarry was in sight, at which point it was unleashed to pursue the deer.

Big game hunters from all over the world came to India to visit the princes and shoot with them. Of course each visitor wanted to get his tiger. Although tigers are plentiful in parts of India, notably the northwest, in other places they were not common at all. Sometimes it was necessary for the hospitable prince to send quietly to Rajasthan for a tiger that could be turned loose and hunted. Emily Hahn, in her charming book on the maharajahs, remarks: "Occasionally a bigwig would come up by rail itching to go and get his tiger while unbeknownst to him the tiger was traveling on the same train up ahead in the van."

When the Prince of Wales (later Edward VII of England) visited India in 1875/76, he hunted cheetah and black buck and engaged in the famous local sport of pig-sticking. In Ceylon he killed his first elephant, and in Nepal he shot his first tiger, a female eight and a half feet long. Few sporting events can ever have been arranged more lavishly than that tiger hunt. For the prince and his party of twenty sportsmen, the High Commisioner of Nepal laid on a thousand riding elephants and ten thousand soldiers to act as beaters and servants. Small wonder that the prince shot six tigers in one day.

By no means all tigers have been shot for sport. Some of the finest trophies in existence are the heads and skins of man-eating tigers shot by professional hunters who received a government bounty. Stories of the stalking of these fearful beasts and of man-eating leopards have been recounted in several classic adventure books by professional hunters including Jim Corbett's *Man-Eaters of Kumaon* and Kenneth Anderson's *Nine Man-Eaters and One Rogue*. Anderson tells of the man-eating leopard of Gummalapur, which "established a record of some forty-two human killings and a reputation for veritable cunning that almost exceeded human intelligence." He terrorized an area of 250 square miles. Many of the beasts have devoured dozens of villagers before hunters succeeded in stalking them to the conclusion of their man-eating careers.

The wild regions of America, especially the Alaskan wilderness, produce notable big game trophies. One of the rarest and most difficult to obtain is the polar bear.

The Alaskan brown bear, or "Kodiak," is one of the finest big game trophies of the North American continent. John Quincy Adams IV's specimen was one of the few to be sold at auction in recent years. Sotheby Parke Bernet Los Angeles

In 1957, *Sports Illustrated* chronicled the successful hunt and kill of a specimen that weighed over twelve hundred pounds. Its skin, which alone weighed over 250 pounds, was "squared" at 11 feet, 2 inches (any hide over 10 feet is considered exceptional).

Another magnificent trophy is the Alaskan brown bear known as the Kodiak, which is the largest living carnivore. The specimen sold in the John Quincy Adams IV sale had been shot at Chinita Bay, Alaska, on 15 June 1948. It stood approximately nine feet and weighed 1,800 pounds. At auction it sold for $1,050, a very high price indeed for a big game trophy.

Typical prices of some other trophies of American origin are:

- Polar bearskin rug: $150
- Brown bearskin rug: $75
- Buffalo (i.e., American bison) head
    with horns 19 inches long: $400
- Grizzly bearskin rug with head, 78
    inches long from tail to nose: $250
    (This is a popular skin; other examples
    sell for $150 to $350.)
- Black bearskins with heads, not
    so popular, selling for around $100
- Dall's Mountain Sheep ram's head,
    length of horn around outside
    of the curl, 34 inches: $150

Aside from the game trophies mentioned, there remain stuffed birds and mounted fish. There is no contest between the two on the score of popularity: the birds are much the more popular. Mounted and shellacked fish, nearly always carrying on their mounts notice of size and of date and place of taking as well as the fisherman, are little sought by collectors; few examples have sold for more than $25. Stuffed birds, on the other hand, although no longer as indispensable as they were to Victorian decorators, are still popular, possibly because

A large American buffalo head with horns measuring nineteen inches. It was sold in 1973 for $400. Sotheby Parke Bernet Los Angeles

The complete skull of the American buffalo (Bison bison). *It was formerly the property of the family of William Jennings Bryan. Note the large bullet hole at the left.* Collection of James F. Carr, New York

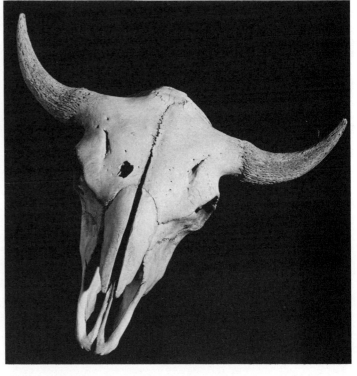

Stuffed and mounted birds include (at left) *a puffin, an Icelandic falcon on a ptarmigan, and* (at right) *a pair of ptarmigans in winter plumage.* Edward W. Sheldon

Pronghorn antelope (Antilocapra americana) *taken in Wyoming. The horns are present in both sexes.* Edward W. Sheldon

Dall's sheep from Alaska. Edward W. Sheldon

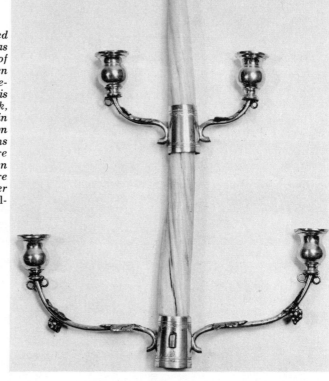

Animal trophies are sometimes converted into small decorative objects as well as "organic furniture." Here the ivory tusk of a young narwhal, 14½ inches long, has been polished and mounted in silver as a candlestick. The narwhal (Monodon monoceros) *is a rare aquatic mammal with a single tusk, occurring only on the male. It is found in polar waters. The tusk on a full-grown animal measures six to eight feet. The horns that found their way to European treasure cabinets in the Middle Ages were then thought to be those of unicorns and were regarded with awe. These unsigned silver mounts are probably twentieth century.* Collection of James F. Carr, New York

taxidermists excel at making them retain a lifelike appearance. Some typical prices in this category are:

- Chinese ring-necked cock pheasant in
full summer plumage, mounted: $40
- Pair of sea gulls in Victorian glass
case: $25
- Pair of goosanders, mounted: $50
- Victorian glass case, 3 × 5 feet,
containing an assemblage of 32
stuffed birds: $100

Some trophies of sport have been neither stuffed nor mounted. Objects of the most varied nature have been made with or from animal relics. The nineteenth century was a prime era for the construction of such objects. A Victorian silversmith, for example, could take the hoof of a favorite deceased pony, set it in a silver mount, and make an inkwell for the owner's desk. In some respects the Victorian mind was quite far from that of the present day. Lady Dorothy Nevill, a student of art, a collector, and a person of the most refined sensibilities, tells

Antlers have been used to make furniture for the last two centuries. This settee was sold at auction in 1973 for $350. The back is flanked by a pair of elk antlers and the whole rests on elk-hoof feet. The upholstery is simulated zebra skin. Sotheby Parke Bernet Los Angeles

proudly in her memoirs of her devotion to a Siamese cat, one of the first introduced into England. When her pet died, she had it skinned and the skin made into a muff, which she constantly used. "I still have a memento," she writes of the cat, "in the shape of a muff made from her coat, very much resembling beautiful sealskin, which it is usually taken to be." Such a trophy would surely appeal to few cat fanciers today.

Victorians used animal relics in the manufacturing of jewelry such as tiger-claw pins and elk-tooth trimmings for watch fobs.

As mentioned, antlers might be made into lighting fixtures in Victorian times. A classic example of using animal remains is the Victorian umbrella stand made from an elephant's foot, but elephant feet have also been used in more recent times in ways just as extraordinary—as the bases for cocktail tables and other bar furniture.

Even more striking is furniture that incorporates parts of animals into its structure. The most familiar type of this furniture, which is sometimes referred to as

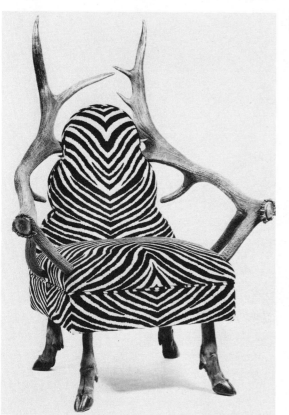

A chair made with elk antlers, sold in 1973 for $200. Sotheby Parke Bernet Los Angeles

"organic," is the chair with a back, arms, and legs made of antlers or horns around a leather seat. Such "organic" furniture is said to have been known back in the eighteenth century, but it is especially associated with the late nineteenth century American West. Theodore Roosevelt had at Sagamore Hill several chairs made from steer horns, and Western hunting lodges were full of this furniture. Good examples are rare on the market today.

Among the more peculiar aspects of the "1920s style" was the use of exotic animal skins and ivory inlaid into chairs, on the writing surfaces of desks, and on footstools and other small pieces of furniture. This use is identified with certain Parisian furniture makers of the twenties, in particular, Emile-Jacques Ruhlmann, who incorporated sharkskin, ivory, and other unusual substances into his special-order furniture.

Made for the luxury trade, and indeed usually commissioned, this furniture has always been exceedingly rare and expensive.

Ivory from various animals has been used to create both objects of art and the most banal knickknacks. The Victorians, living in the great age of elephant hunting, were very fond of ivory and used huge quantities of it in making decorative objects. In 1892, Sir Mountstuart Grant Duff, a Victorian diarist who himself had been a colonial official, noted that the London market absorbed the ivory of about eight hundred elephants each year. Walking-stick handles, parasol handles, card cases, sewing cases, snuffboxes, glove fasteners, billiard balls, and many similar small items were carved from it.

Elephant ivory has always been the most desirable, but objects have also been carved from the teeth of the hippopotamus. Hippopotamus ivory is hard and white, and in Victorian times was favored for umbrella handles. Japanese netsukes were often made of dolphin's-teeth ivory and also from sperm whales' teeth. Nineteenth-century scrimshaw was usually carved from whales' teeth.

A large percentage of the "ivory" on the market in antique shops today is actually plastic. Although the collector might assume that it is easy to tell the difference between animal ivory and contemporary plastics, the differentiation in a well-made piece can in fact be quite difficult. Objects of Far Eastern manufacture and with Far Eastern motifs, including figurines and net-sukes, are especially suspect. Some of the plastic "ivory" figurines are made in Italy and then finished in Taiwan or Hong Kong. Bone has also been passed off as "ivory," since ivory has always been more desirable and expensive.

The Vince Lombardi Trophy given for World Professional Football Championship by the National Football League, made by Tiffany & Co. The National Football League. Photograph from Tiffany & Co., New York.

5

AWARDS

In the Olympic games of ancient Greece the winners were awarded only a crown made from the leaves of the wild laurel. It was the honor of the victory rather than the prize that was supposed to count. When the athletes returned to their home city-states, however, most sources agree that they were presented with "many valuable gifts." These may be considered the first sports trophies.

The word trophy signifies a memorial of a victory. It is used not only for the spoils of the hunting field but, by extension, for objects more or less made for the occasion that are presented to the victors in an athletic competition. It seems unlikely that there is any sport engaged in today, amateur or professional, that does not have trophies to be awarded to the best player or team.

Awards can take many forms—trophies, medals, ribbons. In bullfighting the trophies are parts of the slain bull. At the end of the fight a matador is awarded such parts on a regular fixed scale understood by him, the spectators, and the judges. The reward for a good fight is one ear; for an excellent fight, both ears; for a superlative fight, both ears and the tail, too. Only very rarely is the supreme trophy, a hoof, awarded. Its presentation indicates a perfect fight from start to finish. The spectators wave white handkerchiefs to indicate to the judge which of these awards they want given to the fighter. The music played during the awarding of the trophies is the triumphant tune known as "La Diana."

A prize is a form of award that is not an object manufactured for the occasion like a trophy—a sum of money, for example. Jewels were often presented to winners in the past. At a shooting match in New York City in 1749, each marksman paid twenty shillings to enter. The prize for which they competed was "a large rose diamond ring, value sixteen pounds."

Trophies are often called "cups," and in sports writing the two words are generally used as synonymous. The reason for this is a good historical one: from the seventeenth century on, many trophies in the English-speaking world were, in fact, cups. The two-handled form was often used. Probably the original intent was that the victor could be toasted in "loving cup" fashion, each handle being grasped. A glance at a sports page in any newspaper will show that the words *cup*, *cup winner*, and other derivatives are continually used in this sporting trophy sense. Trophies are also sometimes called "mugs," referring to the one-handled form of cup. The most famous of all trophies, the America's Cup for Yachting, is affectionately known as "The Old Mug."

Trophies are usually thought of now as being made only of metal, but pottery and porcelain have both been used, especially in Victorian times, and at present all sorts of odd objects are used in made-to-order trophies, including—for example—automobile hubcaps. The great bulk of trophies, however, have been silver, gold, or the metals that at first glance give the appearance of silver or gold. The increase in the prices of precious metals has meant that more and more trophies are only sheathed in them or made of other shiny metals.

The longest history of trophies in a sport belongs to horse racing. In Elizabethan times the prizes given to race winners were silver bells. These charming trophies are extremely rare. The city of Carlisle in England preserves two silver-gilt bells given in 1599 to the winners of the races at Kingmoor course. One of them carries the initials of Henry Baines, who was Mayor of Carlisle in 1599, and is inscribed:

The sweftes horse thes bel to tak
for my Lade Dakar sake

which today would read

The swiftest horse this bell is to take
for Lady Dacre's sake

Horse racing became especially popular in the England of Queen Anne between 1702 and 1714. The queen herself instituted a Gold Cup Prize for the Yorkshire races in the first year of her reign. A few of these annual prizes have survived. The 1705 prize, six inches high, weighing twenty-three ounces of gold, is a two-handled cup with cover, engraved with the royal arms. It was made by Pierre Harache, Jr., a refugee Huguenot silversmith from France. Such gold objects are, needless to say, extremely expensive. This 1705 cup has been sold three times at Christie's in London, the most recent price (in 1967) being $75,000.

The Hanoverian dynasty kept up royal patronage of the turf and the tradition has been continued by the English royal family until today, the present queen and her family being themselves actively engaged in racing and jumping. The Hanoverians also gave prizes for races: George I and II bestowed gold teapots on the winners of the annual Edinburgh races. In 1721, the Scottish poet Allan Ramsay composed a verse on this somewhat unusual form of trophy called *On a Gold Teapot 1721*, in which he punningly compared the three heats of the race to the teapot filled three times. Several of these gold teapots have survived; the one most recently sold at auction in London was the 1736 prize, and it fetched nearly $100,000. The English gold cups and teapots are doubtless the highest-priced trophies that ever have been or are likely to be on the market.

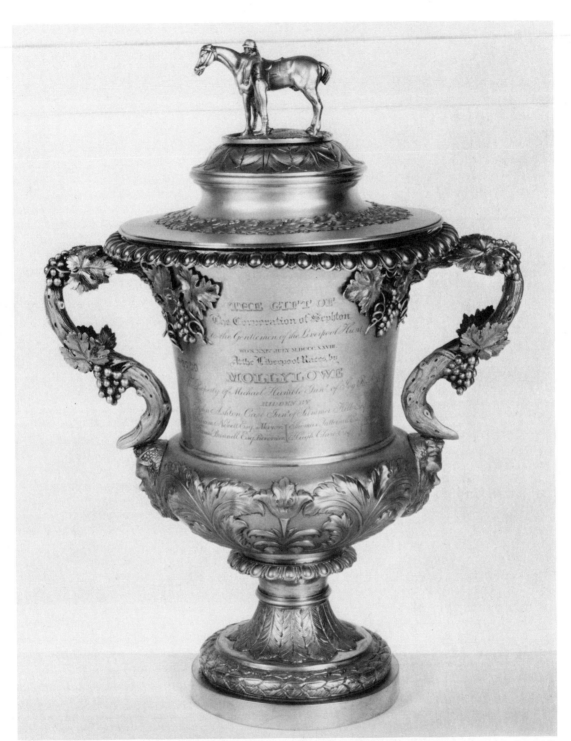

The Corporation of Sephton, England, awarded Mollylowe a silver standing cup and cover by J. E. Teney & Co., 1828, when she won the Liverpool races that year. Note that she was ridden by John Ashton Case, Jr., of Summer Hill, Esq., obviously a "gentleman rider" rather than a professional jockey. Sotheby's Belgravia, London

Queen Victoria kept up the Hanoverian tradition of presenting cups to winning horses in important races, such as those in Guernsey in 1843, very early in her reign. Sotheby's Belgravia, London

The America's Cup races of September 1974 were commemorated with an etched pewter plate, 10¼ inches in diameter, made in an edition of 1,000. Reed & Barton

Tiffany & Co. were the makers of the late-nineteenth-century Commodore Morgan Cup for Sloops. Photograph loaned by James F. Carr, New York

The tradition of expensive materials cast into simple designs, such as teapots, for trophies faded out with the eighteenth century. Under the "Adam" influence toward the close of the century the "cup" gradually became more of an "urn," reflecting the classical orientation of the time. By the middle of the nineteenth century trophies had become exuberant in their design, loaded with more or less appropriate motifs. Although cups or urns continued to be made by the thousands, trays, boxes, and various kinds of standing objects became increasingly popular. The New York Yacht Club Regatta prizes for 1871, for example, included "The Commodore's Challenge Cup for Sloop," and another for schooners, but for other races a water pitcher, vase, cigar stand, and two punch bowls were awarded.

Yachting was one of the first sports to become noted for its trophies. The first record of cups being given to the winners of yacht races is recorded in a peculiarly titled work by Joseph Strutt, *Glig-gamena Angeldeod, or, The Sports and Pastimes of the People of England* (London, 1801). There it was noted that the Cumberland Club annually gave silver cups as prizes for sailing.

The America's Cup was named for the yacht *America*, victor in a race with British yachtsmen around the Isle of Wight, and was given by its winners to the New York Yacht Club as "a perpetual challenge cup for friendly competition between foreign countries" on 22 August 1851. Previously it had been known as "The Royal Yacht Squadron 100 Guinea Cup." It is twenty-seven inches tall with a circumference of thirty-six inches. In addition to its nickname "The Old Mug," it is also called "The Unfillable Flagon." In 1951 when it was lent to the Festival of Britain, leaving the United States for the first time, it was insured, according to the newspapers, for $75,000.

Tiffany & Co. also designed the Astor Cup, which was raced for by schooners off Newport. Photograph loaned by James F. Carr, New York

The silver-gilt Weymouth Regatta Cup was made in London by Rebecca Emes and Edward Barnard in 1827/28. The height is 15½ inches. Victoria and Albert Museum. Crown Copyright

The British style of sports trophy was carried all over the world. Edward Barnard & Sons made an amphora-shaped presentation vase in 1871 for the horse races in Colombo, Ceylon. It was sold in 1974 for $300. Sotheby's Belgravia, London

In Australia a trophy of W. Edwards of Melbourne, made about 1865, was presented to champion cricketers. Note the equipment reproduced in silver on the base. Sotheby's Belgravia, London

The Doncaster Cup for 1859, valued at 300 sovereigns (about $1,500), was won at the Doncaster races by Lord Stamford's horse Newcastle. Made in silver by Hunt & Roskell of Bond Street, London, it was referred to as "an Etruscan vase." Classical references are to the Roman origin of the city of Doncaster. The upper part was removable so "that which before was simply an ornament becomes useful as a claret cup."

Between 1870 and 1951, the America's Cup was defended sixteen times. Sir Thomas Lipton tried five times to win it in yachts always named *Shamrock*, numbers I through V, over three decades from 1899 to 1930. T. O. M. Sopwith, chairman of the British firm of Hawker Siddeley Aircraft, tried twice for the cup, in 1934 and 1937. In 1974 an Australian challenge was beaten by the American entry in the race off Newport, and the cup remained at the New York Yacht Club.

One of the peculiarities of Victorian and Edwardian trophies is that they were called "cups" by almost everyone and yet many were not in cup form at all but were freestanding three-dimensional sculpture. For that matter, it is even quite common for them to make no reference at all to the sport they honored, outside a few lines of engraving. The "Goodwood Cup" given in 1867 to the winner of the well-known horse race held near Chichester since 1802 was described as a

group of statuary in silver, representing "The Death of Harold" . . . The fallen King of Saxon England lies mortally wounded at the Battle of Hastings, when a Norman archer plucks the arrow from the wound and shows it to the Conqueror, who has just ridden up; the victorious standard of William is that instant unfurled.

All of which seems an odd commemoration of a horse race.

Other trophies contained a wealth of topical allusions worked out in precious metal. In the early years of this century long-distance automobile racing was a daring, time-consuming, and expensive sport. Robert Guggenheim gave a spectacular trophy, "The Guggenheim Prize," for the New York to Seattle automobile contest of 1909, which contained five hundred ounces of gold and silver and cost $2,250 to make. Forty-two inches high, it was embossed in high relief with views of Seattle, totem poles, polar bears, busts of Indian chiefs (with Chief Seattle prominent), and other North-

The Chesterfield Cup for 1869 was described by The Illustrated London News as "a classic centre-piece, in silver, designed, with a view to its utility and taste, to hold flowers or fruit." The tazza at the top is glass. The sculpture illustrates scenes from the Iliad.

The Ascot Prize plate for 1871, manufactured by the firms of R. S. Garrard (still in business) and Hunt & Roskell. The plate consisted of a large shield ("The Ascot Cup"), a tankard ("Queen's Stand Plate"), and the equestrian group ("The Royal Hunt Cup"), which represented Henry VIII hearing the news of the execution of Queen Anne Boleyn.

The Country Club of Westchester, the Meadow-brook (Long Island) Club, and the Morristown (New Jersey) Club presented this trophy in 1893 to Henry L. Herbert, for his achievements in polo playing. Photograph loaned by James F. Carr, New York

The 1872 Household Brigade Steeplechase Cup, 31 inches tall, manufactured by Widdowson and Veale. The handles represented the colors of several regiments; the cover is surmounted by an officer of the Horse Guards.

west Coast motifs. Below the name of the cup and on the base were a wreath of laurel and gold sprays holding a large nugget of Alaskan gold and the words "Alaska-Yukon-Pacific Exposition" spelled out in Alaskan gold nuggets.

This sort of rampant overdecoration annoyed some designers of the time who were developing the "modern" style and wanted to simplify trophy making along with the other decorative arts. In the *Art Journal* in 1898 the accomplished "modern" silversmith C. R. Ashbee denounced elaborate trophies and called for refinement in design.

Athens gave her athletes a crown of olive [*sic*; it was laurel], but we give ours a badly spun and intrinsically useless lump of silver, upon which we inscribe names and dates in the various types selected from a printer's catalogue. My plea here is that the Trophy shall be regarded as a work of art ...

He wanted to humanize the entire field, and he preached against the big trophy firms that manufactured "machine-stamped tankards, pencil-cases, and butter spoons."

The pronouncements of Ashbee and other advocates of the streamlined had some

An early-twentieth-century trophy given to the victor in the Harvard-Yale track meet is typical of the less ornate trophies that succeeded the overwhelming decoration of the Victorian era. Photograph loaned by James F. Carr, New York

Abstract design in contemporary trophies —the Hennessy California Cup, made of sterling silver on an ebonized wood base, designed by Tiffany & Co. to be awarded for powerboat racing. Hennessy & Co. Photograph from Tiffany & Co., New York

Conventional motifs are still being employed in sports trophies. Tiffany created the Martini & Rossi trophy for the National Power Cruisers Championship given in 1960 to the American Power Boat Association. Martini & Rossi. Photograph from Tiffany & Co., New York

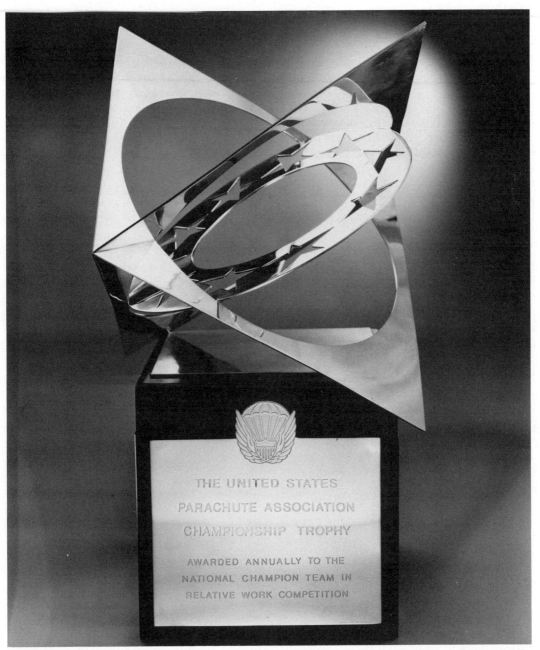

Tiffany & Co. designed the United States Parachute Association championship award, given annually for jumping. The sterling silver trophy is on an ebonized wood base. The ten stars in a circle represent ten parachute jumpers who free fall, holding hands to form a perfect ring, and land with accuracy, symbolized by the cross planes. United States Parachute Association. Photograph from Tiffany & Co., New York

effect. The best trophies of the 1920s and 1930s, done in the style we now call "Art Deco," were simple yet spectacular. They were much closer to the sculpture of the time than previous generations of trophies had been. At the same time, the old-fashioned trophy continued to be made although even it was much less heavily embossed and decorated (rising costs of craftsmanship and metals probably had as much to do with that trend as the art of design did). Of course many of the most famous trophies still held by players and clubs were made in the nineteenth century or earlier in this century.

The trophy industry flourishes today; the growth of nearly every sport has brought a tremendous demand for prizes and awards of all kinds, as a glance at the walls of any country club or even the hall of a high school shows. The world's largest trophy manufacturer is the Dodge Trophy Company, which has six plants that turn out a half-million figures *a month*. These are free-standing trophies, and the company has a line of about three thousand different figures ranging from ponies to Volkswagens, sailboats, patrol boys, rabbits, winged shields, and hundreds of others. At their plant at Crystal Lake, Illinois, the Dodge Company makes the most famous of entertainment awards, the "Oscar," and also the "Emmy" awards for television, as well as the football trophies for the Sugar Bowl, Orange Bowl, and Rose Bowl games.

Mass-produced trophies like these, made to a mold, are not likely to be of interest to the collector, but still being made today are unique trophies or trophies of which there are only a few examples, and these are well worth collecting now.

The subject of trophies as collectible items has been little studied except as a facet of silversmithing, and even then the attention has generally been paid to the silversmith rather than the sport connected with the object. There have been very few exhibitions of trophies. In 1933, a "National Sporting Trophies Exhibition" was held in London—at the time it was said to be the first exhibition of its kind. The most famous English trophy was shown on this occasion. It is a simple urn called "The Ashes," the greatest of all relics of the game of cricket. In 1882 a visiting Australian cricket team defeated the English team. The *Sporting Times* magazine wrote of this defeat as though it were a death and included in the obituary the memorable phrase: "In Affectionate Remembrance of English Cricket, Which died at the Oval on 29th August 1882 . . . N.B. The body will be cremated and the ashes taken to Australia." Some Australian ladies took up the idea humorously and had an urn made containing some ashes, which they presented to England's captain. He in turn bequeathed it to the Cricket Memorial Galley of the Marylebone Cricket Club on the grounds of Lord's, the shrine and mecca of English cricket.

Among the other items on display at this memorable exhibition were trophies won by the sports-minded Prince of Wales (later King Edward VIII and Duke of Windsor), nine for horse races, two for golf, and one for squash rackets. Also shown were such important trophies as the Waterloo Cup for coursing (pursuing hares with hounds), the Westchester Cup for Competition between the United States Polo Association and the Hurlingham Club teams, first played for in 1886, and a magnificent boxing belt presented to the heavyweight champion Jack Scales in 1902.

In the United States only a few trophies are more than seventy-five years old, and those have been awarded in a relatively small number of sports. The oldest North American trophies, generally recognized by sports organizations and halls of fame, are the following (arranged by date):

1851—The America's Cup for
    international yachting
1879—Child's Cup for rowing
1885—International Challenge Cup for
    canoeing
1893—Stanley Cup for hockey

1895—Havemeyer Trophy for amateur golf
1895—McKechnie Cup for Canadian rugby
1895—United States Amateur golf cup
1895—United States Open golf cup
1899—Astor Cup for yachting
1899—Kennedy Cup for rowing
1899—Thorne Cup for western amateur golf
1899—Wadley Cup for golf
1900—Stewards Cup for rowing
1900—Davis Cup for international challenge in tennis

The enormous proliferation of trophies in the United States has come about only in the last fifty years. The National Collegiate Athletic Association, for example, gives championship trophies each year for sixteen different sports. Innumerable other sports organizations give awards; there is even the Owen Churchill National Underwater Spearfishing Trophy, given since 1950.

Many trophies are now designed in the simple "modern" style in the United States, but others continue to be turned out in the flamboyant design technique associated with Victorian times. The Orange Bowl Trophy given in football since 1935, for example, shows a bowl of silver oranges, one of which is peeled to reveal a football player in the forward pass position! The 100th Anniversary Kentucky Derby Cup (1974) was encrusted with diamonds and emeralds and valued at $16,000.

Some trophies in the United States and abroad do not actually leave the hands of the awarding organization. Many are kept in halls of fame or museums of the sport, and only replicas are made for the winners. The Sportsman of the Year trophy given by *Sports Illustrated* magazine is an ancient Greek vase, an amphora of the sixth century. It is kept in the magazine's headquarters in New York, and a replica has been made each year since 1954 for the annual winner. At the Kentucky Derby the owner of the victorious horse is given a gold cup trophy, and silver replicas in smaller size are given to the jockey and the trainer. They get to keep theirs, but the owner does not actually keep his gold cup. The Stanley Cup, which is the oldest trophy competed for by professional athletes in North America, is kept permanently in the Hockey Hall of Fame in Canada. Many hunt cups also remain with the hunt.

Gold and silver trophies have been melted down to recover the metal, and those that are made of base metal have often ended up as mere scrap. Nevertheless, trophies exist on the antique market in great numbers, so great in fact that it is necessary for the collector to be discriminating. The most desirable way to collect is to stick to a single sport and try to accumulate examples of the principal awards of that sport, which are usually given on an annual basis. The best trophies are those that are engraved or have a metal plaque attached to the trophy or its base giving information on winners over a period of time. Much handsome engraving has been lavished on trophies and on trophy plaques, and an extensive history is sometimes recorded. The better trophies—that is, for the most part, those made in silver—are usually hallmarked by the maker. Most of the well-known firms of silversmiths and also jewelers have made and signed trophies. The markings are generally to be found under the base now; older trophies may be marked on the sides.

After trophies such as cups and urns, the most important form of recognition of victory in sports events is the medal. Medals and other decorations to be worn on the person are almost universally appealing. In many Socialist countries they have become a collecting mania that is regularly denounced by the authorities. In Russia, for example, in 1974 it was estimated that ninety-nine state enterprises minted around 100 million *znachki*. These lapel medals or pins are often awarded for athletic prowess as well as for services to the state. In the Soviet Union they are especially prevalent

Medals for the victors in athletic competitions have been distributed by untold millions during the last century. Many are of fine design and craftsmanship, and some have as well a considerable local interest. All the medals shown were awarded by the City of New York at its annual "Safe and Sane Fourth of July Athletic Celebration (or Carnival)" between 1913 and 1930, or worn by officials on those occasions. Most bear the name of the mayor in office with his portrait, the arms of the city, the Statue of Liberty, or some other local emblem, as well as scenes of the sport for which they were awarded. Some of those in the 1918 competition are described as presented by The Mayor's Committee on National Defense. The medals are bronze, sterling silver, gold-plated, and gold-filled. Most bear the name of the manufacturer, Dieges & Clust, which is still in business in New York. Collection of James F. Carr, New York

A sampling of collectible medals, many of them sterling silver, awarded by the United States Olympic Committee at its sports festivals, the 1919 Victory Athletic Carnival, and the Mayor's Committee of Women in National Defense, at events sponsored by now-defunct newspapers such as the New York Daily Mirror *and* Evening Graphic, *athletic equipment companies such as A. G. Spalding, and other organizations between 1913 and 1958. Some of those shown were worn by officials; the winners' medals were the same. Among the sports honored are the broad jump and other track and field sports, baseball, swimming, ice skating, and lacrosse. The makers of most of those shown were Dieges & Clust and Lambert Brothers, both of New York.* Collection of James F. Carr, New York

because of the custom of wearing civilian decorations on civilian dress, and medals are distributed by the bushel. Collecting the innumerable varieties has become a Soviet hobby that the political establishment regards as frivolous.

The modern Olympics give medals to victors, but most sports today award a combination of trophies, medals, ribbons, and cash. Certain sports are particularly associated with the awarding of medals. One of these is sharpshooting, which is also called "marksmanship" or "rifle and pistol shooting." As an Olympic sport it is called simply "shooting." The prevalence of medals in this gun sport is no doubt connected with the fact that so many shooting contests have military origins.

Although shooting contests go back as far as the introduction of firearms into Europe, it was not until the nineteenth century that fine shooting really caught the public imagination and began to be engaged in as a true sport. Marksmanship must be one of the few sports to have an entire opera, and an important one at that, written about it. *Der Freischütz* by Carl Maria von Weber was first produced in Berlin in 1821. Its action both opens and closes on a shooting range.

The sport of shooting became extremely popular in the mid-nineteenth century. In Great Britain the first meet of the National Rifle Association was held in July 1860 at Wimbledon. Queen Victoria and numerous other royalties were present, and the queen pulled a mechanism to fire the first shot and start the festivities. There was a week of firing, which ended with a great ceremony at the Crystal Palace, where a Scottish military marksman was awarded the Queen's Prize of two hundred fifty pounds and a gold medal before more than twenty thousand "English men and women assembled," one commentator remarked, "in that glass palace to take their share of this truly national undertaking."

In the United States the National Rifle Association, formed in 1871, standardized the rules for the sport, which now includes rifle, pistol, and revolver shooting. The first international rifle-shooting match was held at Creedmoor, Long Island, in 1874, matching the United States with an Irish team (the Americans won 934 to 931).

Trapshooting had its beginning in Great Britain at about the same period. Live pigeons were used as targets until the 1880s, when the "clay pigeon" (made of silt and pitch) began to be thrown from a mechanical "trap" for the shooter. The "pigeons" simulated the flight of game birds. The Amateur Trapshooting Association, organized in 1900, has held its "Grand American Tournament" annually since that year.

The sport of skeet shooting came a few years later. In skeet, the trapshooting hurling contrivance is used, but the "pigeon" is hurled in a fixed circular path forty yards in diameter; there are also some other differences from trapshooting.

The second half of the nineteenth century was the period of the giants in displays of marksmanship. Glass balls were the usual targets, although live pigeons were used in exhibitions until about 1900. One of the champions was Capt. A. H. Bogardus. In 1869, he killed 500 pigeons in 528 minutes. A few years later he gave an exhibition in Madison Square Garden at which he shot at 5,000 glass balls in eight hours and twenty minutes, using two guns and employing a man to cool off the guns in a bucket of ice water. He broke 4,844 balls.

One of the most popular entertainers of the age was a famous shot—Annie Oakley. She traveled for seventeen years with Buffalo Bill's Wild West Show and appeared before Queen Victoria (who enjoyed her act) and innumerable other royalties. Annie could shoot the center spot out of a five of spades dropped from a flagpole! She once broke 100 clay birds in less than seven minutes. This remarkable "shootist," as the newspapers delighted to call her, came on in the Wild West show riding a loping Indian pony, shooting targets thrown in the air, shooting flames off a revolving wheel of candles, and shooting glass balls. In a match with royalty she beat the Grand Duke Michael of Russia, a notable shot, forty-seven out of fifty to his thirty-six, and she once shot a cigarette out of Kaiser William II's mouth—at his request.

Many relics of this remarkable woman have been preserved, including guns, medals, and even the glass balls she used as targets. In recent years a number of these items have been sold at auction in Sotheby's Los Angeles galleries.

Some of the amateur shots of the period could pull remarkable feats. The British Lord Walsingham, considered one of the finest shots in his country, on a day in August 1888 accounted for 1,056 grouse. This day's sport took place at his shooting box in Yorkshire, which bore the incredible name of Blubber House. His granddaughter relates that she once saw Lord Walsingham bring down a bird while he was crossing a stile with his gun under his arm. Lord Walsingham's other favorite pursuit was entomology, in which he obtained great distinction; his lepidoptery collection of moths and butterflies is now in the British Museum.

On the continent the Archduke Franz Ferdinand, who was killed at Sarajevo, was a notable shot who practiced his sport in all parts of the Austro-Hungarian Empire to which he was heir. On a single day in the Bohemian forests he once accounted for 1,630 pheasants, hares, and rabbits.

The Amateur Trapshooting Association's Permanent Home Grounds at Vandalia, Ohio, are the scene each August of the "Grand American Tournament." In recent years, over a nine-day period more than two million shotgun shells have been fired by forty-five hundred participants. In the tradition of Annie Oakley, women are still outstanding in this sport. In 1950 the Grand American was won by an eighteen-year-old girl named Joan Pflueger, who broke one hundred straight clay pigeons.

Shooters' medals like military medals generally have the conventional round shape and are suspended from a ribbon. Frequently they bear a metal or enamel reproduction of a rifle. Nineteenth-century medals were made of bronze, silver, or (surprisingly often) gold. Since many of these were won by men in military service, their inscription will read something like "Given to the Best Shot in so-and-so Company." Fine examples, even in gold, are generally available at under $100. The medals given by rifle and revolver clubs and other shooting organizations are usually silver or bronze; they are less expensive. It is desirable that any of these awards be preserved with the original ribbons.

The numerous medals given in other sports, particularly in swimming and track and field events, are interesting collectibles that are frequently priced at no more than $5 to $10. The skill of the medal maker was often considerable, and in addition the backgrounds with local scenes add to the interest of a collection. A good sampling of these medals is shown on pages 108 and 109. A collection can be formed with a very modest outlay, around one sport, one athletic organization, or one locality. Sterling silver is indicated by those words on the medal. "GF," which appears on a number of those shown, means "gold-filled"; "gold-plated" is not generally indicated.

The traditional trophy in boxing since at least the middle of the nineteenth century has been the championship belt. Before that time boxers fought, quite frankly, for cash prizes, which were sometimes—by the standards of the day—extremely large, as much as one thousand pounds in England. There were no generally recognized championships or any particular standards—the Marquess of Queensberry's rules date from 1865, but did not become universally accepted until 1889. There were also no gloves, and the fights were often bloody in the extreme. At the famous encounter between the American John C. Heenan and the Englishman Tom Sayers at Farnborough, England, on 17 April 1860, both fighters were described as "bathed in blood"

A large number of trophies are "perennials"—that is, the same object is awarded each year, and the winner keeps it until he is defeated. It has long been customary for the names of the winners to be inscribed on the trophy, as was done between 1870 and 1879 on the Monmouthshire Gun Club Challenge Cup, made by Stephen Smith in 1865. Sotheby's Belgravia, London

after the two hour and twenty minute fight (thirty-seven rounds). The referee called the fight a draw and *both* contestants were awarded championship belts.

Boxing belts are generally about 2½ inches wide, made either of black leather with an engraved buckle or of metal plaques showing scenes of boxing, national coats of arms, and other symbols, and of course the name of the championship. The engraved plaques are about four inches long. The collector interested in boxing history can usually get a nineteenth-century leather belt and buckle for under $200. Those that consist of metal plaques are more expensive, and most expensive of all are the solid gold belts that have been made on occasion. The gold belt awarded to Dick Smith when he became the first light-heavyweight champion of Great Britain in 1918 was sold at auction in 1966 for more than $1,000. Other gold or bejeweled belts have undoubtedly changed hands for much more money.

Reproductions of trophy belts and buckles or buckles alone are being made today. The belts of course are made of leather, the buckles brass or sometimes sterling silver.

Many professional sports players have enjoyed relaxing with another sport. This is George Herman "Babe" Ruth, greatest of baseball players, on his return from a pheasant-shooting expedition in the 1920s. Museum of the City of New York

6

SPORTS MEMORABILIA, AUTOGRAPHS, AND PHOTOGRAPHS

MEMORABILIA

Seeking out and holding onto memorabilia of teams and players is the admiring, emotional, and affectionate side of sports. The spectator sports of today are producing more collectible memorabilia and more collectors than the sports of individual achievement ever have; this is a rapidly expanding aspect of collecting antiques of sport.

"Fan" memorabilia is gushing out at an astonishing rate for the millions of fans of a great variety of sports. When Yankee Stadium in New York City began renovation in 1973, there was such a tremendous demand for souvenirs of that historic field that the company in charge of the renovation sold lockers, uniforms, seats, ticket drums, and other equipment on a department store scale. Managements have become very alert to the fans' craving for souvenirs and, not content with selling memorabilia actually used as the above items had been, are manufacturing and distributing new products. Encouraging the collecting of memorabilia is, of course, a way to augment attendance in an era when there is increasing competition among sports as well as teams. A good example is related to the Yankee Stadium renovation: each member of the audience at the final day of the 1973 season at the stadium, the last one before the renovation commenced, to see the Yankees play the Detroit Tigers (the Yankees lost, 8 to 5), was presented with a long-playing phono-

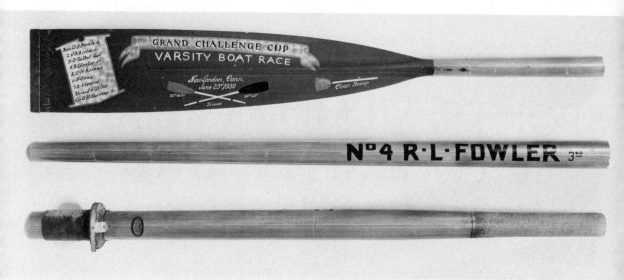

Memorabilia of a sport should always have as much documentation as possible. This unusual piece of sports memorabilia, which is an oar (now cut into three sections), was used by Robert Ludlow Fowler of the Harvard crew at the Varsity Boat Race at New London, Connecticut, on 23 June 1939 and later at Henley. The documentation includes a photograph of Fowler in his crew sweater, a scrapbook showing the Yale-Harvard race of 1940, which Harvard won, and a program. The same crew rowed in England at the Henley Royal Regatta in 1939, which was the centenary year of that most famous rowing event, and won the Grand Challenge Cup. The page from a scrapbook kept by Fowler at Henley shows the various heats in progress. Fowler was killed in action at Guadalcanal in 1942 and awarded the Navy Cross posthumously. Collection of James F. Carr, New York

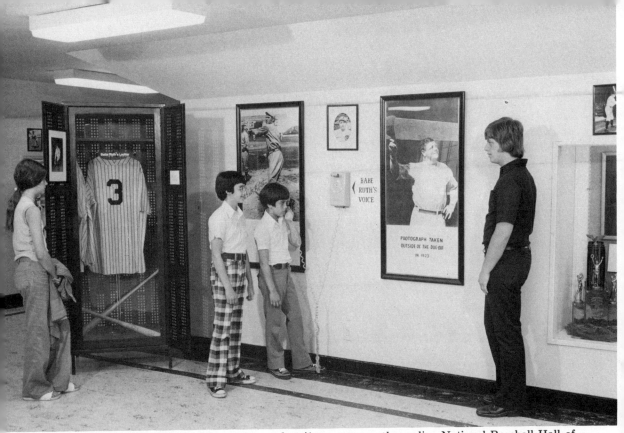

The Babe Ruth Wing displays his locker and uniform among other relics. National Baseball Hall of Fame and Museum, Inc.

graph record especially made for the day, entitled "Great Moments at Yankee Stadium." Since there were 32,238 fans present, collectors will probably find a good many of these available for years to come.

Every sport will have relics of a famous performer, usually human, but not always. Among the more exotic relics of racing is the skeleton of the horse Lexington. Although he ran in only seven races (of which he won six) in the years 1853 and '54, this Kentucky stallion at stud became the "greatest sire of thoroughbred running horses America has ever produced." He died at the age of twenty-five in 1874, having begot over two hundred winners. His mounted skeleton is now kept in the Museum of Natural History of the Smithsonian Institution in Washington, D.C.

Among personal relics of sport, many of which are museum treasures today, preserved because they were the property of well-known people, are such curiosities as the hawking glove of King Henry VIII of

England. Made of "shamoyed" leather (meaning dressed as a chamois skin would be) and embroidered with red and blue silk and silver thread, it is now kept in the Ashmolean Museum, Oxford.

The modern idea of preserving relics of people specifically noted as sportsmen— Henry VIII, after all, had other claims to distinction—goes back no further than the great sportsmen of the nineteenth century. When "Nimrod" died in France in 1843, his saddlery and kindred properties were sent over to London and sold as relics at an auction at the Baker Street Bazaar.

Today, sports figures are as honored by shrines and museums as are the famous achievers in other fields. In 1974, a Babe Ruth Birthplace Shrine and Museum opened in Baltimore, for example. The growth of the "hall of fame" dedicated to the best players of a particular sport is a good indication of a new trend toward honoring sports heroes. Museums of various sports also encourage this kind of collecting,

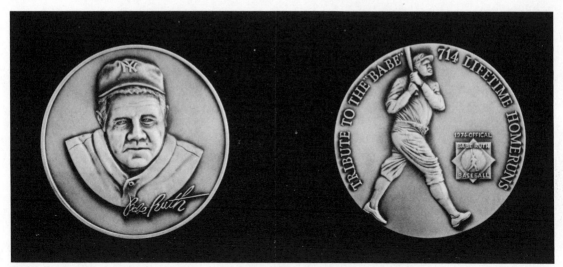

Babe Ruth, who batted sixty home runs in the 1927 season and was twelve times home run leader in the American League, was honored in 1974 with this medal issued by Babe Ruth Baseball, a sports organization for young people. Medallic Art Company, Danbury, Conn.

since they often house the equipment and other personal possessions of outstanding players.

Among the new halls of fame is the Lacrosse Hall of Fame Foundation, Inc., in Baltimore. Lacrosse is a New World game, first played by the Canadian Indians and passed by them to the French settlers. It became an organized sport by 1860, when the rules of the game were standardized. It is one of the few sports to have an official national standing; in 1867 the Canadian Parliament adopted lacrosse as the national game of the country. In about the same era it gained a following in the United States. The antiques collection at the Lacrosse Hall of Fame includes equipment used by the Indians, old wooden sticks, and a 1906 Harvard uniform containing, as the curator says, "some original Cambridge mud!"

Among the important halls of fame are the following:

The National Lawn Tennis Hall of Fame and Tennis Museum, Newport, Rhode Island

Hall of Fame of the Trotter, Goshen, New York

Indianapolis Motor Speedway Museum, Indianapolis

The National Museum of Racing, Saratoga Springs, New York

United States Ski Hall of Fame and Ski Museum, Ishpeming, Michigan

Pro Football Hall of Fame, Canton, Ohio

Very few of these halls date to earlier than the 1950s, when the idea of a permanent hall of fame for various sports caught on among fans; local authorities had by then realized that such museums would be great tourist attractions. As of 1974, there were nearly forty of these institutions, and others had been announced for the future. In addition, some large collections of

The National Museum of Racing and Hall of Fame is located in Saratoga Springs, New York, a center for racing since the 1860s. The Travers, first run in 1864 at Saratoga, is the oldest stakes race in the United States. National Museum of Racing, Inc., Saratoga Springs, New York

Some of the collections of the National Museum of Racing—paintings, trophies, and, in cases (foreground), the silks of famous jockeys. National Museum of Racing, Inc., Saratoga Springs, New York

sports memorabilia and trophies are open to
the public, such as Citizens Savings Hall in
Los Angeles, which maintains halls of fame
for twenty different sports, including badminton, fencing, gymnastics, handball, soaring, weightlifting, and others, each with its
trophies.

The most elaborate establishment devoted to the athletes of a single sport is the
National Baseball Hall of Fame and Museum at Cooperstown, New York, opened in
1939. Abner Doubleday's baseball is preserved there, as are the trophies and mementos of Babe Ruth and the shoes, sweater,
and other baseball belongings of Ty Cobb.
Innumerable mitts and masks, gloves, bats,
uniforms, and even lockers used by celebrated players of the sport are to be found
in its collections.

It comes as no surprise that the game of
baseball has the most flourishing shrine.
This American game has particularly knowl-
edgeable and sentimental fans and even a
Society for American Baseball Research,
among whose active membership are fans
who specialize in the statistics of minor
leagues and similar esoteric knowledge. One
member has compiled a directory of every
home run ever hit by a major league player.
At the present time baseball is certainly far
in front of the other spectator sports, even
football, in the devoted accumulation and
study of memorabilia. In that respect, if no
longer in size of attendance, baseball is still
the national game. In 1973, the "First Annual Baseball Nostalgia Exposition" was
held in Chicago, and thousands of enthu-
siasts traded baseball cards, programs, magazines, scorecards, autographs, and other
memorabilia.

During the renovation of Yankee Stadium, pictures of famous players who had
appeared there were sold for from $150 to
$350. Blown-up photographs were also sold
to fans, including one of Don Larson's last
pitch in his 1956 perfect World Series win
over the Brooklyn Dodgers and one of
Hank Bauer sliding home in the 1953 series.

Bats commemorating winning teams and
carrying the names of all players on a team
for the season have been manufactured by
various baseball equipment companies.
These sometimes reproduce the actual signature of each player. The Hillerich &
Bradsby Co. of Louisville, Kentucky, for
example, issued a "Louisville Slugger 125"
bat with the signature of the World Championship New York Mets team of 1969.

Bats manufactured with facsimile signatures of famous hitters are nothing at all
new, and the collector should beware of
thinking that a signed bat, even a quite old
one, is an actual relic of a famous player.
The 1912 A. G. Spalding & Brothers catalogue lists such bats for sale—at $1.00 each!
—with signatures of Larry Doyle, Harry H.
Davis, Frank W. Schulte, and many others.
The note in the catalogue describing these
is of interest in showing how old this idea is:

In order to satisfy the ever increasing demand from our customers for bats of the
same models as used by various prominent
National and American League players, we
have obtained permission from some of them
to include in our line duplicates of the bats
which they are actually using and which
we supply them with, and these "Players
Autograph" bats, bearing the signature of
the player in each case, represent their
playing bats in every detail.

Much more dazzling souvenirs than bats
have been produced for special baseball
events. An elaborate bronze ashtray in the
form of Shea Stadium, New York, was manufactured for presentation at the 1964 dedi-
cation of the field. Members of the winning
World Series teams receive a memento, usually a ring today. That awarded to the 1969
"Miracle" New York Mets was heavily
embossed with a view of Shea. Such souvenirs, for obvious reasons, are seldom on
the collector's market, but if found are
among the handsomest of baseball memorabilia.

Other specially created baseball souvenirs
include personal season passes made of various metals. These date to the early 1900s.

In recent years the autographed football has joined that perennial collectible, the autographed baseball. Here is an official-sized National Football League ball signed by members of the Minnesota Vikings before they played in the 1974 Superbowl game. The signatures are facsimiles. The Gallery, Amsterdam, New York

Commemorative editions are being made to honor nearly every sport. On Deck, a bronze baseball sculpture by Jay O'Meilia, was cast in 1973 in an edition of fifteen. The height is 13½ inches. American Gallery of Sports Art, Dallas

(That was also the era of the personal metal pass on railroads, at opera houses, and other places where the prominent were to be distinguished.) The baseball passes measure about three by four inches, somewhat larger than the ordinary paper ticket of that day. A 1900 Cincinnati baseball season pass in pewter was engraved with the date and a scene showing a patron entering the turnstile. Another for the Cincinnati season of 1902 was made of sterling silver and engraved with a scene of the ball park with pennants flying. Each of these rare items was valued at $300.

Baseballs autographed by outstanding players or an entire team are one of the prime collectibles of the sport. Entire auctions have been held of signed baseballs. The collection of Alphonse J. Leveque, consisting of more than four hundred baseballs autographed only by players in the World Series and dated 1927 to 1969, was sold at auction by the Plaza Galleries in New York in 1973. The balls included both team-signed balls and those with individual player signatures. The George M. Rinsland auctions in Allentown, Pennsylvania, have specialized in the sale of autographed baseballs.

Some typical prices for autographed baseballs sold during the 1970s are:

- Ball signed by most members of the 1915 Phillies Club: $80
- Ball signed by 15 players of Connie Mack's 1930 pennant-winning Philadelphia team: $100
- Ball signed by St. Louis Cardinals of 1930: $55
- Ball signed by the World Championship New York Giants of 1933: $45
- Ball signed by players (26 signatures) in the "Old-Timers" game, Philadelphia, 21 August 1953: $125
- Ball signed by the New York Yankees 1937 World series team, including Lou Gehrig and Joe DiMaggio: $155
- Ball signed by Babe Ruth and Goose Goslin: $130
- Ball signed by Dizzy Dean and 15 other players: $25
- Ball signed by Casey Stengel, Sandy Koufax, and 13 other players: $50
- Ball signed by Babe Ruth, Ty Cobb, and 14 other players: $125
- Balls signed by nonchampionship teams or by lesser-known players, around: $10

The autographed photograph of a sports celebrity is more widely collected than almost any category of autograph. This is the golfer John Farrell, who won the United States Open tournament in 1928 and was made a member of the Professional Golfers' Association Hall of Fame. Photograph loaned by James F. Carr, New York

AUTOGRAPHS

Autographs of sports interest written on paper rather than on baseballs constitute an area of specialization that is an older and more serious type of collecting than the amassing of recent memorabilia. It is also quite accessible both to the beginning and the advanced collector, as it offers a wide range of prices. For our purposes here, the material may be divided into autograph letters and manuscripts; signed photographs; and signatures on programs, philatelic items, and other paper.

The collector who keeps his eyes open for autographs relating to a particular sport is often rewarded by finding a letter or document by a well-known person relating to his special enthusiasm. This statement is of course truer of the more ancient sports such as hunting than it is of quite recent sports like baseball. An entire collection has been formed, for example, of letters and manuscripts by famous people mentioning the game of tennis, the earlier items (before about one hundred years ago) referring to the indoor game, court tennis.

A sampling of letters and manuscripts of

typical sports interest includes such items as:

- A letter on vellum dated 8 August 1621 from King James I of England, one of the country's huntingest monarchs, to his Master of the Game Thomas Lumsden authorizing him to destroy any roving greyhounds that threaten the deer on the royal preserves in Yorkshire: $150

- A letter written in Florence in 1716 from Marco Antonio de Mozzi to his friend Francesco de Frescobaldi discussing the game called *il calcio*. This is the famous game played in Tuscany from the Middle Ages on, which is the direct ancestor of present-day football: $20

- Manuscript journal kept by Frederick John Staples-Brown, 1867–75, recording runs with staghounds, foxhounds, and harriers in the counties of Berkshire and Shropshire, illustrated with pen-and-ink sketches. 92 pp.: $125

- Manuscript program of the races at Epsom, England, listing prize money, the class of horse, handicaps, etc., in May 1777. 1 page: $125

- President Theodore Roosevelt, keen for so many sports and writer of a staggering number of letters, is a fine source for the collector's quest. The following are typical:

Letter, 1879, asking for otter skins:	$350
Letter, 1908, about the best kind of hunting socks for African trip:	$160
Letter, 1911, about climbing Mount Katahdin, Maine:	$100
Letter, 1910, about hunting in East Africa:	$120

- Ernest Hemingway engaged in and wrote about many sports. He was also a prolific and flamboyant correspondent. Typical of his letters, which bring high prices from collectors, are:

Letter, 1949, on prizefighting:	$170
Letter, no date, on fishing:	$275
Letter, 1959, on bullfighting:	$525

- James J. Braddock, heavyweight champion of the world, letter, 1940: $20

- Clyde Beatty, animal trainer, letter, no date: $25

- Walter Camp, football coach, letter, 1922: $20

- Rogers Hornsby, baseball player, letter, 1933: $15

- Ty Cobb, baseball player, canceled check, signed: $20

- Knute Rockne, football coach, 1920 letter about scholarships at Notre Dame: $75

- Roger Maris, baseball player who hit sixty-one home runs in 1961, on printed chart of runs with name of each pitcher he homered off: $50

Photographs autographed by one's favorite athlete are not a twentieth-century invention. They date back to the latter part of the nineteenth. The earliest photographs that were suitable for autographing were the *carte-de-visite* type, which were popular in mid-century, and athletes are to be found among the subjects as well as statesmen, royalty, actresses, and other persons of note. Not until the spectator sports that attract large numbers of fans began to be organized in the late nineteenth century did photographs signed by sports figures begin to appear in large numbers, however. In the twentieth century the "glossy" photograph, usually 8 × 10 inches, has been the popular form, and those signed by noted athletes and sportsmen have a very wide currency among collectors. The best, of course, are those autographed to a specific collector or friend and done in person by the athlete—signed photographs of an especially noted figure have sometimes been broadcast by his agent. A sample of 1970s prices shows that this familiar form of memorabilia can command rather substantial figures:

- Annie Oakley, markswoman,
     signed in 1906: $100

- Lou Gehrig, baseball player,
     inscribed with message: $100

- Babe Ruth, baseball player: $60

- Johnny Bench, baseball player: $10

- Mark Spitz, swimmer: $15

Programs, scorecards, and annuals are among the printed items most often presented to players for their signature. Typical prices for such items are:

- Scorecard signed by Babe Ruth: $40

- *Connie Mack's Baseball Book*
     (1950), signed by the author: $35

- 1969 Atlanta Braves *Yearbook*,
     signed by 26 players next to
     their pictures: $20

- 1969 New York Mets *Yearbook*
     (their championship year), signed
     by 27 players next to their
     pictures: $30

In recent years there has been great interest in getting the signatures of well-known sports figures on philatelic material. There are thousands of sports stamps. The American Topical Association publishes a checklist that gives sports and recreation stamps issued by various countries, showing nearly every sport engaged in today. Collecting sports stamps is the fourth most popular category with "topical" stamp collectors (after animals, space, and Americana). Some of the statistics in this list are

extraordinary: it is difficult to believe, but true, that twenty-two countries have issued a total of forty-one stamps depicting the sport of water polo, or that twenty-seven stamps have been issued by eighteen countries to honor handball. An entire collection could be formed of shot-put stamps, since at least eighty-four stamps have been issued by thirty-nine countries in that category.

The most popular philatelic item is the "First Day Cover," a special envelope prepared for the first day the stamp is issued. The sports commemoratives in this category are ideal for the collector to have autographed by a player. Since a great many stamps connected in some way with sports have been issued in recent years by the United States, there is now an "FDC," as they are called, for nearly any sport a collector wants.

Here are samples, with typical prices:

- Physical Fitness Stamp FDC signed
     by Mark Spitz, swimmer: $10
- James A. Naismith Basketball
     stamp FDC signed by eight members
     of the National Basketball Hall
     of Fame: $25
- Football Stamp FDC signed by ten
     members of the Football College
     Hall of Fame: $25
- Traffic Safety FDC signed by Dan
     Gurney, racing car driver: $10

The National Baseball Hall of Fame sells postcards of the bronze plaques dedicated to players in the hall. Collectors like to have their favorite baseball hero sign the postcard showing his plaque. These are valued at $10, more for especially noted players.

Although this book does not deal with printed matter relating to sport, the ubiquitous "sports card" cannot be ignored in mentioning memorabilia. Collecting these cards was a juvenile pastime that, like so many other areas of collecting in recent years, has become a very busy adult avocation. The American Sports Card Collectors Association opened its first annual show in New York City in May 1973 (there are many other organizations and shows). At that time the nonsports cards issued in cookies, candy, chewing gum, and other juvenile-oriented products were at a low premium among collectors. Cowboys, for instance, birds, movie stars, and other subjects were considered much inferior to the sports subjects. The best cards were baseball, then boxing, football, basketball, and hockey.

Sports cards have been issued for nearly a century with cigarettes, cigars, newspapers, marbles, soft drinks, bakery goods, cornflakes, candy, and (especially) chewing gum. It was calculated that in 1972 about one billion cards were issued, the Topps Chewing Gum Company of Brooklyn alone accounting for about 250 million baseball cards. Topps began issuing cards in the late 1940s, and by 1955 they were supreme in their field and had a virtual monopoly. Baseball players then formed a union and signed a collective contract with Topps for the reproduction of their portraits on cards. Each receives an annual stipend. The 1973 Topps set of cards consisted of 700, which were sold in packs of ten cards with a piece of bubble gum for ten cents or twelve cards without the gum for the same price.

As in every collecting field that depends on printing and photographic reproduction, it is the errors that make value. The players' feats, reputation, looks, and so forth have little to do with the desirability of a card and the high price of some. A 1910 card showing Eddie Plank, who pitched for the Philadelphia Athletics, was quoted in 1973 at $300 because the engraver's plate for this card broke, and copies are rare. A price of $100 was quoted for another 1910 card issued by Sweet Caporal Cigarettes showing a little-known Boston Braves player named Bill Sweeney because the markings and the letter B on his uniform had not been printed in red as they should have been.

Each field of collecting has its great rarity. In that same 1910 series, which appears to have been jinxed, a card was issued honoring John Peter (Honus) Wagner, a shortstop for the Pittsburgh Pirates who was elected to the Baseball Hall of Fame in 1936 and called then "the greatest shortstop in baseball history." He sued the cigarette company for reproducing his picture on one of their cards because he was an opponent of smoking. The card had to be recalled by the manufacturers. There were, of course, survivors, fourteen in number according to some calculations. The card was thought, in the early 1970s, to be worth about $1,500. Honus Wagner was also portrayed in the Baseball Caramel series. This card is not rare; he had nothing against candy. At the same time the cigarette card was quoted at $1,500, the candy card was estimated at $2.

Of little favor among card collectors is the Leaf Gum Company, which in the 1940s conceived a scheme whereby it skip-numbered its card sets (1, 2, 3, 6, 7, 9, etc.) so that kids aiming at complete sets (which all did) would go on buying bubble gum forever seeking the nonexistent cards.

For a collector today to have 500,000 sports cards is not unusual. There are many publications, reference and periodical, devoted to the lore of the hobby, which seems to inspire its followers, adolescent and adult, with singular enthusiasm. Collectors have been known to buy cornflakes and other products by the case just to get the cards.

Souvenirs of baseball teams are not going to become rare very quickly. Among the list of official souvenirs sold by a typical baseball team at stadium stands or by mail order are pennants (in various sizes), pen and pencil sets, sunshades, sweatshirts and T-shirts, paperweights, beer glasses, cigarette lighters, key chains, letter openers, dolls, caps, and rings, all marked with the name of the team, of course, and usually a logo as well.

SPORTS PHOTOGRAPHS

An emerging field for the collector interested in antiques of sport is the photography of his favorite sport. Great opportunities still exist in this area for the collector of modest means—every flea market and innumerable antiques and junk shops have stacks of old photographs and also photograph albums that sell today for a few dollars.

The great difficulty in collecting old photographs is always the problem of identifying the subjects. The sitters and places photographed are seldom identified by name on the photograph itself; a high proportion of all the old photographs found today are quite anonymous as to subject. For the sports-minded collector, however, this lack of personal identification is not too serious a drawback. If the sport being engaged in is completely obvious, the photograph probably belongs in his collection—it will perhaps show some variations in the way the sport was once played and will illustrate old equipment and the costumes worn by the players. A collection of early photo-

Stereoscopic views include many delightful sporting scenes. Series were issued that in their entirety tell a complete story. Two views published by George Barker of Niagara Falls, New York, in 1887 show hunting scenes: "Dragging in the Deer" and "Getting Supper Ready." Complete series on sporting

Fishing schooner racing between American and Canadian vessels is depicted in this series of medals (both sides are shown). The races were held between 1920 and 1930. The medals, 1½ inches in diameter and designed by Harry Lawrence Gage, were issued in 1973 to celebrate the 350th anniversary of the founding of the port of Gloucester, Massachusetts. Medallic Art Company, Danbury, Conn.

subjects are a good area for specialization in sports antiques. Because most were entered for copyright, the views are generally dated. Pinney Collection

Underwood & Underwood, one of the most famous nineteenth-century American photographic firms, made this stereoscopic view of "Miss Ward, Greatest of all Lady Divers" in 1889. Note that the view is called "Instantaneous," a process that came in with the stereoscope and made possible a broader range of action photographs. Pinney Collection

graphs of baseball, tennis, bicycling, shooting, and other sports can be formed relatively inexpensively.

The majority of the photographs in such a sports collection will not be particularly old. Today, everyone is so accustomed to seeing innumerable illustrations of sporting events in newspapers and magazines in a single day that it is difficult to realize photography, speaking in terms of antiques, is a quite recent development. Action photography, in general, is less than one hundred years old. Showing a sport or indeed any event in progress was virtually impossible for the camera before about 1880, when the famous experiments of the Anglo-American photographer Eadweard Muybridge in showing motion brought new dimensions to picture taking. It is particularly interesting to the collector that the Muybridge experiments were largely concerned with sports of various kinds. "Instanta-

neous" photographs are known to have been taken outdoors as early as the 1850s, but the results of these few attempts are seldom to be found.

Before the 1880s there were millions of daguerreotypes, tintypes, ambrotypes, and photographs of all kinds produced all over the world. The *carte-de-visite* photographs, popular after 1860, were cards about 2½ × 4 inches with the photograph of a sitter centered and a margin that could be signed. They were originally used as calling cards. Photographs of celebrities, political and theatrical especially, were made in almost unbelievable numbers by enterprising photographers and sold to the public—in fact, the photograph of anyone in the news who would sit for his photograph was available on a *carte-de-visite*. Naturally, famous athletes were included. Pugilists topped the list, as they were so much in the news in the mid-century at the time of the celebrated

Bowling played with a varying number of pins (it was sometimes known as "ninepins") is an ancient game in the United States, having been introduced into New Amsterdam by the Dutch in the seventeenth century. It became an organized sport in the late nineteenth century, when this New York team was photographed. Photograph loaned by James F. Carr

Opposite page
Duke's Cigarettes card from the series "Yacht Colors of the World": about 2¾ x 1½ inches. The series included some fifty or more cards each picturing an actress dressed in the colors of a particular organization—here, Kate Vaughan in the colors of the American Canoe Association. Pinney Collection

A group of tennis-playing friends in Missoula, Montana, in 1889. The backdrop is of local scenery although the photograph is a studio one. Note the court outfits and also the size of the early tennis rackets.

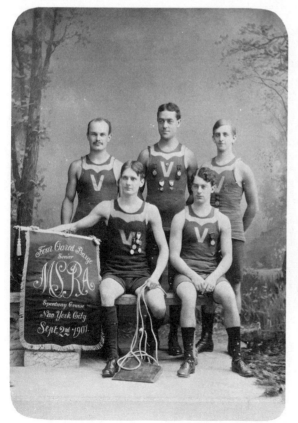

Rowing became an organized sport very early in the United States. The Castle Garden Amateur Boat Club in New York City was organized in 1823. The first intercollegiate event has remained the most famous—the Yale-Harvard Regatta, first held in 1852. The crew pictured here, as may be seen from their banner, were victors in a 1901 event. Photograph loaned by James F. Carr, New York

Opposite page

The 1893 champion football team at Trinity School in New York City. Photograph loaned by James F. Carr, New York

Heenan-Sayers fight of 1860. Other sports figures were pictured on *cartes-de-visite* and, a little later, in the larger "cabinet" photographs, but all these were indoor studio portraits showing the notable in nonsports surroundings with at most a piece of his equipment, such as a hunter with his gun or a trophy. The most common photographs then, and those most commonly available now for collectors, are of people who combined a sport with show business like Annie Oakley or, at an earlier period, the famous lion tamer Isaac Van Amburgh, of whom there is a daguerreotype as early as about 1850. Even in those early days some of these celebrities were astute enough to sell the rights to reproducing their physiognomy (in the case of the pugilists, generally a battered one) to one special photographer from whom they drew a royalty. Not all the sports figures shown were human—portraits of famous horses, nearly always racehorses or trotters—were made too and reproduced in the thousands.

A strange phenomenon of the 1860s was the "composite photograph," which was made from more than one negative or from a combination of photographs and drawings. The earliest known "composite photograph" in America has a sports connection—it includes a famous racehorse, Dexter. According to Robert Taft, the historian of photography, this was produced in 1867:

An "instantaneous" photograph of Dexter in motion was made and enlarged. A number of photographs of individuals were taken as "bystanders" and prints of the horse and the bystanders cut out and pasted on a prepared painting.... The whole thing was then re-photographed and prints made.

It was photography of motion, again involving horses, that was responsible for the famous experiment of 1872 by Eadweard Muybridge (his name was really Edward Muggeridge but he thought the other spelling more "Saxon"). This changed the history of sports photography, as it led directly

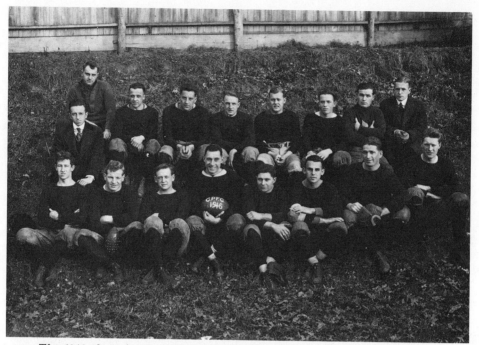

The 1916 champion football team at College Point, New York. Photograph loaned by James F. Carr, New York

Early photographs of bullfight scenes are quite rare. This one was taken by Dr. William H. Keller (shown on page 63), *an American visitor, at Madrid on 12 May 1890. It shows the farewell fight of the bullfighter called "Frascuelo." Keller annotated the photograph to show that he paid $15 for a seat "sombra delantera." Seats at bullfights are sold "sol" (sun) or "sombra" (shade). The sombra are naturally more desirable. "Delantera" means "in front."* Photograph loaned by James F. Carr, New York

The American woman bullfighter Conchita Cintron is shown in this photograph fighting on horseback. Photograph loaned by James F. Carr, New York

into the "action" photograph so prevalent today. In 1872, Leland Stanford, millionaire railroad builder and former governor of California, bet a racing acquaintance that, when a horse was galloping, there was a point at which all four of its feet were off the ground. To prove his point, he commissioned Muybridge to make a series of photographs of the horse in motion. This involved many cameras, hundreds of exposures, and a large outlay of money, but at the conclusion Muybridge's photographs proved that a galloping horse does indeed have all four feet bunched and off the ground simultaneously.

In the history of sporting art, this new fact was of the greatest importance. It showed that the classic "rocking horse" motion portrayed by thousands of painters, in which the horse runs with its front feet stretched forward and its rear feet stretched backward, was in fact incorrect. Some horse painters are said to have taken to their beds at this news. Muybridge went on experi-

menting with photographs of horses and humans in motion in Philadelphia under the auspices of the University of Pennsylvania. In 1887, he published eleven volumes with over 700 plates showing human bodies, many nude or lightly clothed, in motion. Male nudes are shown engaged in various sports, including riding, fencing, and pole vaulting. The Muybridge photographs have had great influence in photography. They have been studied by many artists, including the contemporary English painter Francis Bacon, and those showing sports action are now very much collectors' items. Although the complete Muybridge books sell for several thousand dollars, individual plates are often available.

After 1880 photography began to encompass every sport, indoor or outdoor. In 1881 a sensation was created at a photographer's convention by a photograph showing three tennis balls in midair. At the same time, stereoscopic views were made showing

Faireno being led in by his owner William Woodward after winning the Lawrence Realization (first run 1889) at Aqueduct, New York, in 1932, T. Malley up. Photograph loaned by James F. Carr, New York

sportsmen, such as hunters stalking game. In the 1890s, fine photographs were made of skating, cycling, golf, archery, croquet, polo, even netting wildfowl and hawking. Great sports events were shown: the Henley Regatta, cricket at Lords, and Ranelagh polo in England; the Kentucky Derby, the Vanderbilt Cup road races, and the World Series of Baseball (after 1903) in the United States.

Many photographs of sports have not only their period charm but importance as documents of social history. Photographs have been used to verify the history of sport. The history of the introduction of lawn tennis into the United States is documented by early photographs showing it being played on Staten Island. It was brought there by Mary Ewing Outerbridge, who set up the first court in America. She had become acquainted with the game in Bermuda, where it was a new fad, and obtained net, rackets, and balls from the British officers stationed there. It was first played in the United States in 1874 on the grounds of the Staten Island Cricket and Baseball Club (the site is now occupied by the tollbooths of the Verrazano Bridge). The first national tournament was played at the island's Walker Park Tennis Club, which still exists, on 1 September 1880.

Few antiques of sport offer more enjoyable study than the photographs of the late nineteenth and early twentieth centuries. Many discoveries about the history and practice of various sports have been made, and more doubtless will come. Fortunately, such photographs are still easily obtainable and not costly. Stereoscopic views, for example, are commonly sold between 25 cents and $1.00 today (1975) when they are printed on paper. Those on glass, which were

Two scenes of American steeplechasing early in the century. "Going to the post" at the Rose Tree Fox Hunting Club, Media, Pennsylvania, and a view of the spectators in high fashion of the day. Pinney Collection

mostly produced in a brief period between about 1855 and 1865, are rarer and much more expensive, up to $25 each. Views that have been colored, views of certain geographical areas (the Far West, for example), and of certain historical events (the Civil War) are among the most expensive categories, but, so far, those of sports interest have remained in the lower price range. As for twentieth-century sports photographs, unless they are prints of the work of a very noted photographer they are still sold in batches today with prices averaging only a few cents. There are exceptions, of course, of which a good example is contemporary photographs of famous prizefights.

The history of baseball is shown in memorabilia of all kinds and in the photographic record at the baseball museum in Cooperstown. National Baseball Hall of Fame and Museum, Inc.

7

NEW PATHS IN SPORTS COLLECTING

New paths for the collector of antiques of sport strike out in many directions in addition to those already mentioned in the text or captions. The equipment of dozens of sports is still collectible today for modest sums. In addition, the costumes required for various sports have recently begun to attract collectors. Museums are showing interest in the many special outfits that have been produced for sportsmen (and spectators) not only in the more distant past but in this century. The Smithsonian Institution has acquired ski outfits (complete with skis) from the 1930s, golf suits of the 1920s, along with the wood-shafted golf clubs of that era, and sports-car caps of the mid-1950s. Other museums have sought the "bloomer" outfits introduced for women's gymnastics in the 1880s, which had great influence on the role of women in sports because, although cumbersome and enveloping by today's standards, they made possible an entirely new range of activity just by fitting loosely.

If the collector wants to research an antique find, chances are it can be documented. Record keeping seems to be the very essence of sport. Some records are ancient almost beyond belief. The Marathon track event run today at the Olympic Games is the same 26 miles 385 yards run from the battle of Marathon to Athens in 490 B.C. The distance is also that of the Boston Marathon, which has been run annually since 1897.

Hunting records go back to the Middle Ages. As for modern sports records, a glance at the pages of innumerable "sports encyclopedias" and "sports almanacs" will show a wealth of detailed statistics. A baseball encyclopedia recently published contained nearly a million and a half baseball facts, including a chronological list of teams from 1882 on, with the name of every single professional player in the history of baseball in the United States, even those who played in a single game. The science-fiction writer Isaac Asimov once predicted that in fifty years computers could be so programmed with baseball probabilities that the "game" would be "beat the computer."

Cricket is well documented from the eighteenth century to the present. England's most famous player was W. R. Grace, born in 1848 and died in 1915, a surgeon by profession but such an avid cricketer that he gradually gave up his practice. During his cricket career, which began in 1864, it is known that he scored exactly 54,896 runs and took 2,876 wickets. The information gathered on this game has even been used in research that has nothing to do with sport. A diligent scientist used cricket statistics to study the cycle of sunspots. His studies showed that English cricket batsmen tended to hit 3,000 in a single season— a relatively rare event—more often in years of maximum sunspot. Because the wicket— the part of a cricket field on which the ball is thrown and bounced to the batsmen—

would tend to be "sticky" (i.e., wet) during rainy weather, the conclusion is that summers of sunspot maximums would tend to have lots of dry, sunny weather. Also, fewer games would be canceled during sunny weather, and so more runs would be scored in such a season.

The iconography of sports is possibly even more extensive than their written documentation and can be of great assistance to the antique collector. The dimensions of the field are immense. Sporting subjects in paintings, sculpture, and prints constitute, in fact, one of the major themes of Western art. It is worth pointing out that in addition to numerous artists such as Arthur Devis, John Ferneley, and Sir Alfred Munnings, who are classified as "sporting artists," many other famous artists also have painted or sculpted sporting subjects. They include—among popular nineteenth-century French painters, for example—Gustave

Courbet, who painted *After the Hunt* (Metropolitan Museum, New York), Eugène Delacroix, Honoré Daumier, and Pierre Auguste Renoir. One of Renoir's most charming paintings shows young ladies playing battledore and shuttlecock. Manet painted a portrait of a lion hunter showing the hunter with his gun and the dead lion. Even Georges Seurat painted a sport—the principal figure in the celebrated *La Grande Jatte* (Art Institute, Chicago) is a woman holding a fishing rod.

As for sporting prints, there must be no sport that is not depicted in them. The great period of the sporting print was the early nineteenth century, coinciding with the development of the aquatint medium, which is especially suited to rendering outdoors effects. Racing, hawking, shooting, fishing, cockfighting, boxing, and other sports were depicted. Today engraving, etching, silk-screening, and other techniques are used to produce prints of these and more modern sports.

Among the sports not previously discussed that offer promising antiques for the collector are these:

TENNIS. Lawn tennis partially descends from the old indoor game called "court tennis," but its invention is generally credited to Major Walter Clopton Wingfield in 1873. The major, who was English, combined various features of games already played, such as the net from badminton (which was originally an Indian game called Poona; it took its English name from the home of the Duke of Beaufort, where it was first played, also in the 1870s) and the ball from "Eton Fives" (a form of handball). The name of Wingfield's game was "Sphairistiké," after a game of that name supposedly played in ancient Greece—but, not surprisingly, that name never caught on. The inventor patented the outdoor court idea in 1874 and had sets of equipment made by Messrs. French & Co. of 46 Churton Street, Pimlico, London. Herbert Warren Wind has described these sets as containing poles, pegs, nets, mallets, brushes, bags of balls,

and four tennis rackets, made by Jefferies & Mallings, "which were a sort of cross between the conventional hard-rackets racket and the conventional court-tennis racket." The set came encased in a wooden box, 36 × 12 inches, bearing the label "Sphairistiké or Lawn Tennis" on the cover and was accompanied by a little book called *The Book of the Game*. There were three editions of this equipment and the book, but soon players assembled their own equipment from the other games, and the major's sets were off the market. Today, a set would be the foundation of a tennis collection.

Rackets used in lawn tennis and in the other racket games, such as court tennis (by far the oldest, known since the fourteenth century), racquets, squash racquets, and squash tennis, vary in size and somewhat in shape, as well as in balls used.

BICYCLING   A great amount of memorabilia from the early days of this sport remains to be collected today. The original enthusiasm was so great that all sorts of games were thought up—even a bicycle polo, which must have required great dexterity on the wheels, was played in the 1880s. The bicycle clubs mentioned earlier and their "runs" produced many charming souvenirs. They include itineraries of the runs, generally printed on small cards of stiff paper about the size of an invitation on which the details of the run are listed with all the stops for refreshment and rest together with the distances between stops. These cards sometimes acted as stubs, which were punched at each stop to show that the rider had indeed made each of the required stations—generally five to ten—and checked in. Tags for bicycle handles were also issued as well as shoulder patches of fabric, sometimes very handsomely imprinted with the club name.

As to the bicycles themselves, there was little collecting of old specimens until the mid-sixties. In 1964, Sotheby sold a "Penny Farthing" bicycle (the type with an enormous front wheel, in this case fifty-four

inches in diameter) for $185, and in 1966 there was an entire auction of a collection formed by G. Southon, which included such oddities as a "quadricycle" sold for $1,200 and a tricycle for adult riders made in Coventry about 1876 for $1,000. Few collections as large and important as the Southon have reached the market since the sale, but museums are giving great attention to the study of the bicycle along with all other forms of transport. The United States National Museum (Smithsonian) has an excellent collection, and there are good examples in the transportation museums that are opening in many places.

As in all areas of the antique transportation field, the condition of collectible bicycles is extremely important. Collectors prefer, as they do with old automobiles and other vehicles, that as many of the parts be original as possible. Replacements—and the majority of old transport has replacements —should always be of the period. "Restoration" of the condition of the bicycle is not objected to, provided replacements are period and the work has been done with careful attention to authenticity. Skillfully restored bicycles command higher prices than those that are all original but in poor shape. Prices for early bicycles (that is, Victorian) begin at less than $100 and go up to a few hundred. The spectacular models like the famous "Penny Farthing" (called the "Ordinary" in America) always get the highest prices.

The history of the development of the bicycle and the sport of cycling as well as much information indispensable to the collector is set forth in *Wheels and Wheeling. The Smithsonian Cycle Collection* by S. H. Oliver and Donald H. Berkebile, Smithsonian Studies in History and Technology Number 24 (Washington, 1974).

The revival of the sport itself in recent years is clearly going to account for a new generation of collector's items. Jewelry stores have been producing initialed sterling silver trouser clips for bicyclists.

GOLF. The game of golf goes back to the fifteenth century in Scotland, and there are many early mentions of it in old letters and documents. Some very old equipment is known to exist. At Dundee, Scotland, is located the Spalding Golf Museum. The

Opposite page and above

Bicycling had great popularity as a sport during the late nineteenth century, and bicycles were manufactured by the millions. They are beginning to be collected today. The Overman Wheel Company of Chicopee Falls, Massachusetts, made these 1891 "safety" models. Photograph loaned by James F. Carr, New York

Elegant sleighs were popular in the nineteenth century when sleighing was a particularly happy and widespread sport in the United States. Well-to-do people had sleighs for winter just as they had carriages for warm weather. Here is Mark Twain's. Such sleighs are, like all antique forms of transportation, attracting collectors today. Mark Twain Memorial, Hartford, Conn.

oldest item in the collection is an iron club made about 1680 and used by Robert Clark, who is considered the first writer on the game. The oldest code for golf was published in Scotland in 1754, and the oldest prints of golfing subjects are from about that same time. Some of these are mezzotint engravings after portraits that show various gentlemen posed with their golf clubs. The shrine of the game, The Royal and Ancient Golf Club of St. Andrews, Scotland, was founded in 1774.

There is some evidence that golf was played in colonial America. A delightful advertisement in the New York *Royal Gazette* for 21 April 1779 notified "golf players" that as the season for "this pleasant and healthy exercise is now advancing . . . clubs and the veritable Caledonian balls" were being sold at the printer's. The popularity of the game in the United States, however, probably dates more from the 1880s; the earliest known photograph of a golf match in the United States was taken in 1888 on a course at Yonkers, New York.

The equipment used in the nineteenth century consisted of a driver, brassie, spoon, cleek, sand iron, and putter, carried in a bunch over the shoulder—there were no golf bags. Any golf equipment of American origin before 1900 is indeed antique. In more recent times, of course, a huge array of equipment has been manufactured. Some pieces, such as a greens level gauge, tee, turf repairer, and stymie marker have even been made in sterling silver.

The history of the sport is well displayed through antique equipment and memorabilia at the Museum and Library of Golf House, headquarters of the United States Golf Association at Far Hills, New Jersey, which opened in 1972. The evolution of clubs, including the wedge, niblick, and driver, is shown, and there is even a display of illegal clubs such as clubs with moving parts, putters on wheels, and concave-face sand wedges. Among the memorabilia is a collection of clubs donated by winners of U.S.G.A. championships and clubs once played with by Bobby Jones, Francis Ouimet, Arnold Palmer, and other professionals, an entire room of presidential golfing mementos, and the clubs of people famous in various fields—astronauts, for example.

The antiques of sport take numerous and sometimes surprising forms: collections have been formed even of plaster casts of the fists of famous boxers, and there is already some interest in antique surfboards. Those of many famous surfers, including Duke P. Kahanamoku, are preserved in the Bishop Museum in Honolulu. A collection of antique bowling balls can be seen at the National Bowling Hall of Fame and Museum in Milwaukee. Antique skis have been collected in the United States Ski Hall of Fame and Ski Museum in Ishpeming, Michigan. Very ancient skis were made of the bones of large animals. In more recent times they have been made from highly polished woods like hickory, ash, or pine. Now a variety of materials, including metals and plastic, are used. Ice skates were probably also originally of bone; iron skates were introduced in the seventeenth century. Such antiques are of course very rare. Even rarer are early roller skates, which were patterned after ice skates with wheels substituted for the steel blade. This design was quickly obsolete as the skater had to keep moving and could stop only with difficulty. There is a pair of these early roller skates in the Chicago Historical Society. Silver or other metal skate keys, initialed or highly decorated, are not so rare.

Although more skates, ice or roller, have probably been made for adults than children, antique skates of either kind are usually found in toy collections and in shops that specialize in selling antique toys. Few date back earlier than 1900; since they are usually patented or have a manufacturer's name, they are datable. Like all toys and indeed many other antiques of this and the last century, skates are much more attractive to collectors if they are preserved in their original boxes. Skates in reasonably

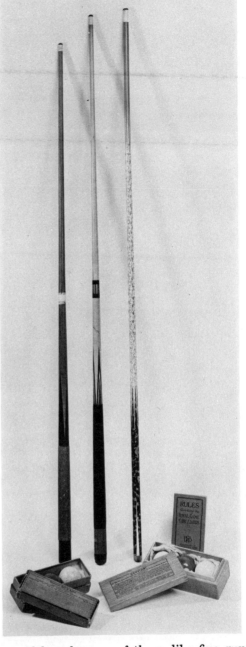

Fine billiard equipment is interesting an increasing number of collectors. Balls made of real elephant ivory such as those shown, which are in their original boxes with instructions dated 1926, are very desirable. The set on the right has never been used. The cues (beginning at left) are hardwood, butt engraved with name of owner, who was Clarence Day, Sr., the "father" of Life with Father *(players kept their marked personal equipment in their clubs in the nineteenth century); a twentieth-century inlaid wood cue with leatherbound grip; a remarkable nineteenth-century cue made in India with brassbound butt, tortoiseshell grip, the stick inlaid and covered with engraved ivory.* Collection of James F. Carr, New York

good condition and of vintage fifty years or more are usually priced at less than $25. The original box premium may double that.

The weapon of the sport of fencing descends from the rapier, a lighter weapon than the sword, introduced about the time that heavy armor declined and firearms were introduced into Europe. From the rapier come the present-day foil, épée, saber, and similar weapons, which developed as fencing ceased to be mortal combat and became an organized sport. If a collector interested in fencing extends his interest back to the rapier, there is a wide variety of collectible items available to him, as edged weapons dating from the sixteenth century on regularly appear on the market. A great many of these are signed by the sword cutler. This area actually belongs to the field of arms and armor collecting, and the collector must seek his quarry at auctions and from dealers who specialize in arms and armor. Foils of the less elaborate kind and not the work of a famous swordsmith, but antique, are often quite inexpensive (under $25). Like all collectible edged weapons, they lend themselves to attractive wall display.

Antiques of most sports can be found by the collector by more or less diligent search-ing. Although some of them, like fine guns, have been collected and studied for centuries, many others, like those pointed out in the last chapter and elsewhere in this book, are only just now coming into their own as collectibles. As interest in sports grows among both participants and spectators, there will undoubtedly be an increase in collecting the artifacts. Antiques of sport is a new and lively field of collecting for many. Often finding the antiques takes some energetic hunting, but then collecting is a sport in itself.

Bibliography

Acton, Harold. *The Bourbons of Naples.* London: Methuen, 1959.

Akehurst, Richard. *Sporting Guns.* London: Octopus Books, 1972.

Allingham, E. G. *A Romance of the Rostrum.* London: Witherby, 1924.

Apperley, Charles James. *My Life and Times* by Nimrod (pseud.), ed. E. D. Cuming. Edinburgh: Blackwood, 1927.

Beaufort, Henry, 8th Duke of. *Hunting.* Boston: Little, Brown and Company, 1885.

Blum, Jonathan. "Wildlife Management and Conservation in East Africa," *Explorers Journal,* Vol. 52, No. 1, March 1974, pp. 27–36.

Durant, John, and Otto Bettmann: *Pictorial History of American Sports.* Cranbury, New Jersey: A. S. Barnes, 1973.

Forbes, Rosita. *India of the Princes.* New York: E. P. Dutton & Co., Inc., 1941.

Forsyth, William H. "The Medieval Stag Hunt," *Metropolitan Museum of Art Bulletin,* March 1952.

Fugger, Nora, Princess. *The Glory of the Hapsburgs*. New York: The Dial Press, 1932.

Genthe, Arnold. *As I Remember*. New York: Reynal & Hitchcock, 1936.

Glasier, Philip. *As the Falcon Her Bells*. New York: E. P. Dutton & Co., Inc., 1963.

Greville, Henry. *Leaves from the Diary*. London: Smith, Elder, 1883.

Hahn, Emily. *The Tiger House Party*. Garden City: Doubleday and Co., Inc., 1959.

Hamilton, Lord Frederic. *The Vanished Pomps of Yesterday*. New York: George H. Doran Company, 1921.

Havighurst, Walter. *Annie Oakley of the Wild West*. New York: The Macmillan Company, 1954.

Hibben, Frank C. *Hunting in Africa*. New York: Hill & Wang, Inc., 1962.

Laver, James. *Victorian Vista*. Boston: Houghton Mifflin Company, 1955.

Love, Paula McS. "Will Rogers' Saddles," *Western Horseman*, May 1953, pp. 37–69.

Magnus, Philip. *King Edward the Seventh*. New York: E. P. Dutton & Co., Inc., 1964.

Mackey, William J., Jr. *American Bird Decoys*. New York: E. P. Dutton & Co., Inc., 1965.

Melner, Samuel and Hermann Kessler, eds. *Great Fishing Tackle Catalogs of the Golden Age*. New York: Crown Publishers, 1972.

Museum of American Fly Fishing. Acquisitions Catalogue, 1969–73. Manchester, Vermont, 1973.

Nevill, Lady Dorothy. *Leaves from the Notebooks*. ed., Ralph Nevill. London: Macmillan, 1907.

Patten, William. *The Book of Sport*. New York: J. F. Taylor Co., 1901.

Peterson, Harold L. *Pageant of the Gun*. Garden City: Doubleday & Co., Inc., 1967.

Pless, Daisy. *Daisy*. New York: E. P. Dutton & Co., Inc., 1929.

———. *Better Left Unsaid*. New York: E. P. Dutton & Co., Inc., 1931.

Richardson, Charles. *The Complete Foxhunter*. London: Methuen, 1908.

Rowse, A. L. *The Elizabethan Renaissance*. New York: Charles Scribner's Sons, 1971.

Steel, Anthony. *Jorrock's England*. New York: E. P. Dutton & Co., Inc., 1932.

Taft, Robert. *Photography and the American Scene*. New York: Dover Publications, Inc., 1938.

Thomas, Joseph B. *Hounds and Hunting through the Ages*. New York: Windward House, 1933.

INDEX

A

Abbey & Imbrie Co., 51
Abercrombie & Fitch, 29, 51, 61
Adams, John Quincy, IV, 74–75, 84
Aitken, Henry, 51
Akeley, Carl, 78
Alexandra, Queen, 22
Alexis, Grand Duke, 27
Allen & Moore Co., 42
Alpine Club, 21
Amateur Trapshooting Association, 111
Amburgh, Isaac van, 131
American Jockey Club, 34
American League (baseball), 120
American Museum of Fly Fishing, 51
American Power Boat Association, 104
America's Cup, 27, 94, 96, 97, 100, 106
Amory, James, 50
Anderson, Kenneth, 83
Anderson Co., 51
angling. *See* fishing
Anne, Queen, 94
antlers, 76, 77, 89, 90
Apperley, Charles James "Nimrod," 21, 42, 117
Aqueduct track, 134
archer rings, 6–8
archery, 6, 16, 23, 25, 134
armor, 33, 143
Art Deco, 106
Ascot Cup, 101
Ashbee, C. R., 102
Ashes, The, 106
Asimov, Isaac, 138
Astor Cup, 97, 107

Atlanta Braves, 124
Augustus III, Elector of Saxony, 18
autographs, 122–23
automobile racing, 27, 28, 118, 124
awards, 93–113

B

Bacon, Francis, 133
badminton, 120, 139
Bailey, John, 66
Baines, Henry, 94
Baker, Sir Samuel White, 78
balloon race, 22
Barker, George, 126
Barlow knife, 69
Barnard, Edward, 98
Barnum, P. T., 74
baseball, ix, 2, 5, 25, 28, 120, 121, 123, 129, 134, 138
baseball bats, 120
baseball cards, 125
basketball, 5, 28, 124, 125
battledore and shuttlecock, 139
Bauer, Hank, 120
Bean, L. L., 61
bearbaiting, 20
Beatty, Clyde, 123
Beaufort, Duke of, 8
Bench, Johnny, 124
Benet, Mrs. B. Pye, 64
Bennett, James Gordon, 2
bicycles and bicycling, 8, 9, 10, 12, 22, 25, 129, 134, 139–40
Bikaner, Maharajah of, 83
billiards, 143

bird decoys, 70
boating, 20, 28
Bogardus, A. H., 110
Boone Hall Stable, 46
Boothby, Thomas, 40
Boss Co., 61
Boston Marathon, 137
Bourgeoys, Pierre le, 59
Bow, G., 9
bowling, 1, 2, 20, 25, 129
Bowman, William, 71
boxing, 16, 19, 20, 22, 25, 27, 28, 111, 113, 123, 125, 136, 139
Braddock, James J., 123
Brainard, David, 68
bridle rosettes, 38, 45, 46
Brocklesby Hunt, 40
Brooklyn Dodgers, 120
Brown, John, 60
Bryan, William Jennings, 85
bull baiting, 16, 20, 21, 22
bull running, 20
bullfighting, 20, 93, 132
Burwash, W., 43

C

calcio, 123
Cambridge University, 6
Cameron, Kenneth M., 51
Camilla Cutlery, 69
Camp, Walter, 123
canoes, 54, 106
Carson, Kit, 62
carte-de-visite photographs, 129–31
Carter, A. & Co., 51
Cartwright, Alexander J., 5
Case, John Ashton, 95
Castle Garden Amateur

Boat Club, 130
Catherine, St., 52
championship belts, 113
Charlemagne, 18
Charles, King of Naples, 16
Charles II, 6
charro outfits, 35–36
Chelsea porcelain, 43
Chesterfield Cup, 101
Chevrolet Co., 4
Child's Cup, 106
Christie's, 94
Chubb, Thomas H., 51
Churchill Co., 61
Churchill Trophy, 107
Cintron, Conchita, 133
Citizens Savings Hall, 120
Civil War, 34
Clark, Robert, 142
coaching, 6, 8, 23, 27
Coalport porcelain, 43
Cobb, Nathan, 71
Cobb, Ty, 120, 122, 123
cockfighting, 15, 20, 21, 22,
    42, 139
Cody, William F., 27
Columbia College, 2
Commodore Morgan Cup,
    96
Cooch Bejar, Maharajah,
    82
Cook, C. C., 26, 39
Courbet, Gustave, 139
coursing, 42, 106
court tennis, 27, 139
creels, 54
cricket, ix, 16, 99, 106, 138
croquet, 2, 5, 23, 25, 134
Cross Rod Co., 51
crossbow, 54–55
Crowell, Elmer, 70, 71
Crowninshield, George, 27
Crystal Palace, 74, 110
Cumberland Club, 97
curling, 25
Currier & Ives, 25

D
Daumier, Honoré, 139
Davis, Harry H., 120
Davis Cup, 107
Day, Clarence, **143**
Dean, Bashford, 55
Dean, Dizzy, 122
Degas, Edgar, 38
Delacroix, Eugène, 139
Derby, earls of, 15–16
Derby, Lord, 23, 40
Derby porcelain, 43

Detroit Tigers, 115
Devis, Arthur, 138
Devonshire, Duke of, 61
Dexter, 131
Dholpur, Maharajah, 83
Diaz, Porfirio, 63
Dickson Co., 61
Dieges & Clust, 109
Dodge Decoy Factory, 71
Dodge Trophy Co., 106
dog collars, 64
dogfighting, 20
Doncaster Cup, 100
Doubleday, Abner, 5, 120
Doyle, Larry, 120
drag hunting, 27
Drais von Sauerbronn,
    Baron Karl, 11
Dudley, Lee and Lem, 71
Duff, Sir Mountstuart G.,
    90

E
Edmonston & Douglas, 45
Edward VII, 23, 61, 83
Edward VIII. See Windsor,
    Duke of
Edwards, W., 99
elephant guns, 61
Emes, Rebecca, 98
Endangered Species Act, 76
Epsom races, 123
Eton Fives, 139

F
Fairbanks, Justin, 5
Faireno, 134
falconry. See hawking
Farlow Co., 51
Farrell, John, 122
fencing, 120, 143
Ferdinand II, Emperor, 55
Ferneley, John, 138
first day covers, 124
fish, mounted, 84
fishing, ix, 2, 6, 20, 30, 139
fishing rods, 50
fishing tackle, 49–54
flies, 52
flintlocks, 57, 59
Foix, Gaston, 16, 42
football, ix, 2, 25, 28, 92,
    118, 123, 124, 125, 131,
    132
Football College Hall of
    Fame, 124
Forsyth, Alexander John,
    59

four-in-hand driving. See
    coaching
Fowler, Robert L., 116
fowling, 20
fox hunting, 21, 25, 27, 28,
    40, 41, 123
Francisco, G. B., 58
Franz Ferdinand, Arch-
    duke, 14, 111
Franz Josef, Emperor, 25
Frederick II, Emperor, 16
French & Co., 139
Frescobaldi, Francesco de,
    123
Friberg, Arnold, 4
Fugger, Nora Princess, 76
Fulton-Barlow knife, 68

G
G & L Sporting Goods
    Store, 62
Gage, Harry L., 127
game trophies, 73–91
Garrard, R. S., 101
gaucho saddle, 36
Gehrig, Lou, 122, 124
Genesee Valley, 41
Genthe, Arnold, 45
George I, 94
George II, 94
George V, 64
Gillie, J. B., 2
Goelet, Ogden, 28
Goelet Prize, 29
Goering, Hermann, 61
golf, 21, 27, 28, 106, 107,
    134, 140–42
Golf House, 142
Goodwood Cup, 100
Gordon-Cumming,
    Roualeyn, 74
Goslin, Goose, 122
Grace, W. R., 138
Grand American Tourna-
    ment, 110
Grand National Steeple-
    chase, 21
Grant, Sir Francis, 41
Grant, Henry, 71
Gravesend track, 39
Greely Arctic Expedition,
    68
Greville, Charles, 15
Greville, Henry, 15
Griswold, Frank Gray, 20,
    27
Guggenheim, Robert, 100
Guggenheim Prize, 100
Gurney, Dan, 124

gymnastics, 120

H
Hahn, Emily, 83
Halford, Frederic M., 52
Hall of Fame of the
    Trotter, 118
Hamilton, Lord Frederick,
    61
handball, 120, 124, 139
Hapsburg family, 12, 15
Harache, Pierre, Jr., 94
harness, 46
harriers, 40, 123
Harvard-Yale track meet,
    103
Hastings, Battle of, 78
Havemeyer Trophy, 107
Hawker Siddeley Aircraft,
    100
hawking, ix, 16, 18–19, 139
Heenan, John C., 111, 131
Hemingway, Ernest, 123
Henley Regatta, 116, 134
Hennessy California Cup,
    104
Henry, Alexander, 60
Henry IV of France, 42
Henry VIII, 117
Herbert, Henry L., 102
Hibben, Frank C., 80
Hillerich & Bradsby Co.,
    120
Hirsch, Baron, 23
hockey, 2, 16, 28, 106, 125
Hockey Hall of Fame, 107
Hofburg Palace, 14
Hofe, Edward vom, 52
Hohenlohe, Alexander, 50
Hohenlohe-Langenburg,
    Kraft zu, 69
Holland & Holland, 61
Holmes, Ben, 70
Hornsby, Rogers, 123
horse antiques, 33–47
horse racing, 16, 20, 21, 25,
    26, 27, 28, 29, 38, 46, 95,
    96, 99, 105, 119, 139
Household Brigade Steeple-
    chase Cup, 102
howdah pistol, 61
Hubert, St., 52
Hudson, Ira, 71
Hunt & Roskell, 101
hunting, ix, 2, 5, 6, 16, 20,
    126
hunting horn, 43–44, 46, 65
hunting knives, 68
hunting swords, 66, 67, 69
Hurlingham Club, 106

I
ice skating, 142
Inburgh, Peter van, 26
Indianapolis Motor Speed-
    way, 118
Instra, 45
ivory, 80–81, 90

J
Jamaica track, 26
James I, 123
Jefferies & Mallings, 139
Jefferson (yacht), 27
John the Good, King of
    France, 16
Jones, Bobby, 142
jumping, 5

K
Kahanamoku, Duke P., 142
Kane, Mrs. Daniel H., 50
Keller, Dr. William H., 63,
    132
Kennedy Cup, 107
Kentucky Derby, 34, 39,
    107, 134
Kentucky rifle, 61
Koehler, Henry, 39
Koufax, Sandy, 122
Kummer, C., 26

L
lacrosse, 118
Lacrosse Hall of Fame, 118
Laing, Albert, 71
Lambert Bros., 109
Lancaster, Charles, 60, 61
Lang, Joseph, 60, 61
Larson, Don, 120
lawn tennis, 23, 25, 27, 28,
    29, 107, 118, 129, 134, 139
Lawrence Realization, 134
Leaf Gum Co., 125
League of American Wheel-
    men, 11
Leonard, H. L., 51
Leopold V of Austria, 65
Leveque, Alphonse J., 121
Lexington, 117
Liechtenstein, Prince of, 25
Lincoln, Abraham, 68
Lipton, Sir Thomas, 100
Litchfield, H. C. & Co., 50
Livingstone, David, 78
Lombardi, Vince, 92
London Coliseum, 6
London Soccer Association,
    2

Lords, 106, 134
Louis XIII of France, 19,
    43, 59
Louis XIV of France, 59
Louis XV of France, 16, 43
Lumsden, Thomas, 123

M
McBride, Sarah, 52
McClellan, George B., 34
Mack, Connie, 122, 124
McKechnie Cup, 107
Mackey, William J., Jr., 70,
    71
MacNaughton, Miss, 2
Madison Square Garden,
    34, 110
Manet, Edouard, 129
Man o' War, 26
Manton, John, 60
Manton, Joseph, 60
Marathon, 137
Marbury, Mary Orvis, 52
Maria Theresa, Empress,
    15
Maris, Roger, 123
marksmanship, 25, 94, 110–
    12
Martini & Rossi Trophy,
    104
Mason's Decoy Co., 71
matchlock, 55, 56
Matterhorn, 21
Meadowbrook Hunt Club,
    34, 102
medals, 107–11
Meek, Jonathan, 52
memorabilia, 115–22
Michael, Grand Duke, 111
Minnesota Vikings, 121
Mitchell, William, 51
Mollylowe, 95
Monmouthshire Gun Club
    Cup, 112
Mont Blanc, 21
Morristown Club, 102
Morse, Peter, 6
Mount Vernon, 50
mountaineering, 21
Mozzi, Marco Anotonio de,
    123
Munnings, Sir Alfred, 138
Muybridge, Edward, 129,
    131–33
Mytton, John, 22

N
Naismith, James A., 5, 124
National Baseball Com-

mission, 5
National Baseball Hall of Fame, 5, 30, 120, 124, 125
National Basketball Hall of Fame, 124
National Bowling Hall of Fame, 142
National Football League, 121
National Horse Show, 34
National Lawn Tennis Hall of Fame, 118
National League (baseball), 120
National Museum of Racing, 26, 118, 119
National Rifle Association, 110
National Steeplechase and Hunt Association, 47
netting, 3, 134
Nevill, Lady Dorothy, 88
New York Giants, 122
New York Mets, 120, 124
New York Racing Association, 26
New York Trotting Club, 27
New York Yacht Club, 97, 100
New York Yankees, 115, 122
Newcastle, 100
Newmarket, 38
Nichols, B. F., 50, 51
Nimrod. *See* Apperley

O
Oakley, Annie, 110–11, 124, 131
Olympic Games, 1, 2, 5, 6, 19, 28, 31, 93, 109, 110, 137
O'Meilia, Jay, 121
Orange Bowl, 106, 107
Orford, Earl of, 22
organic furniture, 90
Orvis, Charles F., 51, 52, 61
Oswell, William Cotton, 78
Ouimet, Francis, 142
Outerbridge, Mary E., 134
Overman Wheel Co., 140
Oxford University, 6

P
Palmer, Arnold, 142
Park Place Croquet Club, 2
Parker, Lloyd, 71
Patten, William, 27

Peel, John, 22
Persimmon, 23
Peterson, Harold, 59
Pflueger, Joan, 111
Philadelphia Athletics, 125
Philadelphia Phillies, 122
philately, 124
Philip, Prince, 8
Phillipps-Wolley, Clive, 23, 73
photographs, 125–36
pigsticking, 42
Pioneer, M. D., 45
pistols, 61
Pittsburgh Pirates, 125
Plains rifle, 61, 62
Plank, Eddie, 125
Plaza Galleries, 121
Pless, Daisy, Princess of, 76
poaching, 12
pocket knives, 68–69
polo, 2, 3, 22, 27, 102, 134
powder horns, 65
Pratt, William C., 71
Princequillo, 46
Princeton, 2
Pritchard Bros., 51
prizefighting. *See* boxing
Pro Football Hall of Fame, 118
Professional Golfers Hall of Fame, 122
punt gun, 61
Purdey, J., 60, 61

Q
Queensberry, Marquess of, 111
Quorn Hunt, 40, 41

R
race walking, 2
racing silks, 38
racquets, 27, 139
Radnor Hunt, 41
Ramsay, Allan, 94
Ranelagh Club, 22, 134
rapiers, 143
reels, 52
Remington Arms, 62, 69
Renoir, Pierre Auguste, 139
Richelieu, Armand, Duc de, 45, 64
Richmond, Duchess of, 78
riding crops, 37
riding the goose, 20
Rigby, 60
Rinsland, George M., 121

Rockne, Knute, 123
Rogers, Will, 35, 36
roller polo, 6
roller skating, 6, 142
Rolls, Hon. Charles, 22
Roosevelt, Theodore, 77, 78, 90, 123
roque, 5
Rose Bowl, 106
Rose Tree Fox Hunting Club, 135
Rousseau, Percival, 63
rowing, 106, 107, 130
Royal Hunt Cup, 101
Royce, F. H., 22
rugby, 2, 107
Rugby Football Union, 2
Ruhlmann, Emile-Jacques, 90
running, 5
Russell, J. & Co., 68
Rutgers, 2, 4
Ruth, Babe, 117, 118, 120, 122, 124

S
saddlecloths, 33
saddles, 34–37, 46
Safe and Sane Fourth, 109
Sagamore Hill, 77, 90
St. Andrews, 142
St. Louis Cardinals, 122
Saint-Simon, Duc de, 59
Salisbury, Lady, 42
Sandalwood, 39
Sayers, Tom, 111, 131
Scales, Jack, 106
Schmidt, Hans, 57, 65
Schulte, Frank W., 120
Schwarzenberg, Princes, 76
Sears Roebuck, 36
Selous, Frederick C., 78
Sephton, England, 95
Seurat, Georges, 139
sharpshooting. *See* marksmanship
Shea Stadium, 120
Sheldon, Edward W., 79
Sheward, William, 50
shooting, ix, 25, 30, 129, 139
shot-put, 124
Shourdes, Harry, 71
shuffleboard, 20
Sibley, R., 43
Sigmund Franz, Bishop of Augsburg, 19
skates, 142
skating, 20, 25, 134
skeet, 110
skiing, 118, 142

skis, 142
sleighing, 141
Smith, Dick, 113
Smith, Samuel and Charles, 60
Smith, Stephen, 112
Snyders, Frans, 66
soaring, 120
Society for American Baseball Research, 120
Solingen, 69–70
Sopwith, T. O. M., 100
Sotheby Parke Bernet, 74, 111, 139
Southon, G., 140
Spalding, A. C. & Bros., 120
Spalding Golf Museum, 140
spearfishing, 107
Spitz, Mark, 124
sporting buttons, 42, 46
sporting guns, 54–66
sports cards, 124
sports clothes, 42
spurs, 46
squash, 27, 106, 139
Staffordshire pottery, 16, 138
staghounds, 16, 40, 123
Stamford, Lord, 100
Stanford, Leland, 133
Stanley Cup, 16, 106, 107
Stanley family, 15–16
Staples-Brown, F. J., 123
Starhemberg, Count Wilhelm, 25
Staten Island Cricket and Baseball Club, 134
steeplechasing, 21, 135
Stengel, Casey, 122
stereoscopic views, 126, 134
Stevens Decoy Factory, 71
Stewards Cup, 107
stirrup cup, 42, 43, 46
stirrups, 46
stuffed birds, 84
Stuyvesant, Peter, 20
Stuyvesant Handicap, 26
Sugar Bowl, 106
Superbowl, 121
Surtees, Robert, 21, 22, 25, 59
Sutton, Sir Richard, 41
Swaine & Adeney, 45
Sweeney, Bill, 125
Sweet Caporal Cigarettes, 125

swimming, 1, 19, 25, 111, 124

T
Taft, Robert, 131
taxidermy, 74, 78
Temple Cup, 30
Teney & Co., J. E., 95
tennis. See court tennis; lawn tennis
Thorne Cup, 107
Thornhill, W., 24
throwing, 5
Tiffany & Co., 29, 92, 96, 97, 104, 105
tiger-hunting, 82–83
Topps Chewing Gum Co., 125
toxophily, 6
track and field, 1, 5, 28, 111
trapshooting, 21, 110
Travers Stakes, 119
Trinity School, 131
trophies, 93–107
trotting, 27, 118
Twain, Mark, 10, 141

U
Underwood & Underwood, 128
Unicorn tapestries, 16
United States Cavalry, 34
United States Open, 107
United States Parachute Association, 105
United States Polo Association, 106
United States Ski Hall of Fame, 118, 142
Updike, A. R., 81
Uzés, Anne, Duchesse de, 77

V
Vanderbilt Cup, 134
Victoria, Queen, 60, 96, 110
Vuitton, Louis, 24

W
Wadley Cup, 107
Wagner, Honus, 125
Waldeman knives, 69
Walker Park Tennis Club, 134

Walsingham, Lord, 111
Ward, Miss, 128
Washington, George, 40, 42, 50, 66
water polo, 124
Waterloo Cup, 106
Watson & Murray, 50
Weber, Carl Maria von, 110
Webb, Matthew, 20
Webster, Sir Godfrey, 78
weighing-in chairs, 40
weightlifting, 120
Welch, Robert, 51
Wells, C. V., 71
Wenger, Maximilian, 56
Wentworth, Lady, 38
Westchester Country Club, 102
Westchester Cup, 106
Westley Richards, 61
Westminster, Dukes of, 40
Westminster Abbey, 78
Weymouth Regatta Cup, 98
Wheeler, C. E., 51
Wheeler, Charles, 71
wheel-locks, 56, 57
Whieldon pottery, 43
whips, 37
White, Stanford, 77
Whymper, Edward, 21
Widdowson and Veale, 102
Wildfowler Decoys, Inc., 71
Wilhelm II, Emperor, 25, 76, 111
William the Conqueror, 78
Wimbledon Hockey Club, 2
Winchester Arms, 62
Wind, Herbert W., 139
Windsor, Duke of, 64, 106
Wingfield, Walter C., 139
Wood, Ralph, 43
Woodward, William, 134
World Series, 134
wrestling, 19, 20

Y
yachting, 25, 27, 97, 106, 107
Yale, 2
Yale-Harvard Regatta, 116, 130
Yankee Stadium, 115, 117, 120
York, Duchess of, 15
York, Edward, Duke of, 16